MODERN TAROT

THE ULTIMATE GUIDE TO THE MYSTERY, WITCHCRAFT, CARDS, DECKS, SPREADS, HOW TO AVOID TRAPS AND UNDERSTAND THE SYMBOLISM

VERDA HARPER

© **Copyright Wryting Ltd 2020 - All rights reserved.**

The content contained within this book may not be reproduced, duplicated or transmitted without direct written permission from the author or the publisher.

Under no circumstances will any blame or legal responsibility be held against the publisher, or author, for any damages, reparation, or monetary loss due to the information contained within this book, either directly or indirectly.

Legal Notice:

This book is copyright protected. It is only for personal use. You cannot amend, distribute, sell, use, quote or paraphrase any part, or the content within this book, without the consent of the author or publisher.

Disclaimer Notice:

Please note the information contained within this document is for educational and entertainment purposes only. All effort has been executed to present accurate, up to date, reliable, complete information. No warranties of any kind are declared or implied. Readers acknowledge that the author is not engaged in the rendering of legal, financial, medical or professional advice. The content within this book has been derived from various sources. Please consult a licensed professional before attempting any techniques outlined in this book.

By reading this document, the reader agrees that under no circumstances is the author responsible for any losses, direct or indirect, that are incurred as a result of the use of the information contained within this document, including, but not limited to, errors, omissions, or inaccuracies.

5 exciting to use Tarot card spreads, covering:

- Relationships
- Mental Health
- Career Challenge
- Self-Confidence
- Self-Care

Get this free PDF quickly so that you can immediately start to work on your newly discovered talent.

To receive your free PDF scan the QR code with your phone camera:

INTRODUCTION

Can you remember the TV adverts throughout the 90s that offered free psychic readings? We would see a caller having their tarot cards read and we would hear shrills of disbelief at the accuracy of the psychic. Millions of people called in, some felt their reading was a life-changing help, despite not being free. Others felt like they had been completely scammed.

Tarot cards have gained a bad reputation through no fault of their own. Luckily, I was already quite fascinated by spiritualism and I had started to appreciate the importance of astrology in Eastern philosophy and in my own life. Because of this, I was more open-minded to the idea of my first tarot card reading, but that's not to say there wasn't still an element of scepticism. Like most teenagers, my friends and I had dabbled in ouija boards, magic spells and tarot cards to decipher our futures. Needless to say, our lack of understanding caused us to read all of the messages incorrectly. In fact, had those experiments with divination come true, I would have become an empress who married a magician, whose name starts with the letters W and N.

"As the poet plays with words, the musician with sounds and the painter with colours, so the tarotist plays with the interaction of tarot cards and the psyche"

— - PHILIPPE ST GENOUX

What a beautiful, yet practical way of explaining tarot reading. Each artist has the tools to create their work. Each type of work brings a sense of peace to the viewer. As a terrible artist with absolutely no ear for music, I decided that tarot would be my art.

My doubts weren't related to the power of the cards. I knew that the symbology was there to help me answer important questions that I needed to figure out the answers to. My concern was more to do with the intricate link to magic and witchcraft. Rather than fall victim to the usual stereotypical assumptions that people make of that which they don't understand, I decided I would open my mind and embrace the unknown.

I had several readings over the space of one year. I wanted to make sure I met with as many readers as possible and with readers of different backgrounds. I wanted to get a feel for how each person interacts with their deck of tarot cards. I suppose that to an extent, I wanted to see if I could spot a fraudster after seeing so many genuinely passionate and caring readers. More than anything, I wanted to draw on the energy of those who either are gifted or have dedicated time to improve their psychic abilities.

We are faced with so many questions in life, so many doubts that seem like there is no right answer. We can spend days, even months, listing the pros and cons of each decision, waiting to see if there will be a better moment, asking friends for advice, or just doing nothing. Even those who are normally quite confident in making decisions will reach a point where the answers aren't clear.

Others feel that there are questions that perhaps they are afraid to ask, but knowing the answers may guide them in the right direction, even prevent them from making mistakes. I know that I went through several stages in my life when I had to ask "Why me?", "What else am I going to have to face" or things like "How am I going to handle this next hurdle?".

In this book, we are going to feed our intrigue as we work through divination practice. We will understand the roots of tarot cards and how they became part of divination. The first part of this book will be about getting to know tarots and the system. We will take a look at the history of tarot and how they have become a tool to help us understand the answers to many of today's difficult questions. I also want to take a little time to bust a few of those myths that are so easy to believe.

We will dedicate a chapter to the reading session. We will look at what you can expect from a reading from a psychic and how to prepare for reading your own cards, or carrying out a friend's reading. You will also need to start learning about what the different colours and images mean, as well as the various spreads or layouts you can try.

Towards the end of Part 1, you can look forward to understanding the relationship between tarot and witchcraft. We will explore the tarot cards that can help you with your spells and some of the extra materials that may also help. After all, as the tenderhearted Aunt Jet Owens said in the movie, *Practical Magic*, "There's a little witch in all of us" and this chapter will help develop the witch or wizard in you.

Once we have an amazing understanding of everything from how to choose the right deck for you to asking the right questions, we will take each tarot and understand their meanings for love, career, and finance. It even matters whether the cards that are drawn display the right way around (upright) or upside-down (reversed), and we will look at the implications of those positions.

I understand how not everyone is ready to believe what the cards are telling them. If you have read my other books, *Healing Mantras* and *Modern Chakras*, you will know that there have been many areas of alternative healing, spiritualism, and the supernatural that I began as a complete non-believer. At no point am I going to tell you what works and what doesn't, as this is down to the individual. I never burn herbs, because the smell irritates me, but that doesn't mean that it doesn't help others. My job is to present my findings in a non-biased way, offer my advice after nearly two decades of experience, and provide you with the knowledge and confidence to enjoy both tarot reading and the relationship with the supernatural.

As always, I want us to have some fun as we are learning and to this end, I will share some of the mistakes I have made along the way, for amusement and in the hope that you don't do the same. Let's begin by understanding what divination is and the role of tarot.

PART I

Prepare to feel like a student again, but if the very idea of that brings bad associations for you, let's clear those away. Here you are studying, of your own free will, a topic that you find interesting and intriguing, and you may find that it brings more improvements to your life than any French or Geography class ever did.

The next few chapters are going to focus on how the tarot cards came to play such a significant role in occult practices. We will start to look at the importance of the Major and Minor Arcana cards, how the suits represent the four elements and the incredible imagery in the cards. We will look at how to use the cards in the right way and how to choose your spread. By the end, you will be shuffling your tarot deck with the right intention, the right question, and the right frame of mind.

Everyone learns in different ways. If only I could read something once and it would be engraved on my brain... Feel free to make some audio recordings of aspects that are important to you and then replay them when you need to, or take a pen and paper and jot down some notes. Some readers may have a little (or a lot) of experience and this will be a great refresher for them. If you are completely new to the amazing world of tarot, I'm really excited for you!

1

UNDERSTANDING THE TAROT

After my year of various readings, I knew that I wanted to learn more about tarot cards and how to read them. It wasn't until I started to carry out my own readings that I began to understand the full scope of the benefits of tarot reading.

If you have read my books on mantras and chakras, you will already know that I have great respect for our own energy and how this energy interacts with the energy of our planet and beyond. By learning how to read the cards, I was able to further work on my energy. Pulling a card lets you take your thoughts and emotions and visualize them as a symbol. In a way, it makes it less personal and easier to separate yourself from everything that isn't helping you in life. You can use the cards to see what energy is holding you back and what is propelling you forward.

On a similar note, putting some distance between yourself and your emotions makes it much easier to see things from different perspectives. tarot cards can tap into your imagination and provide solutions to problems that you may not have considered otherwise. This can really bring about a sense of clarity and peace in your life, something I find is essential for our mental health.

It's true that learning about tarot cards can be a way to help foresee aspects of the future, but really, it is associated with much more than that, specifically, divination. To fully appreciate tarot cards, let's begin with a closer look at what divination is.

WHAT IS DIVINATION?

In very simple terms, we could say that divination is the practice of finding and understanding hidden meanings in events through different techniques, perhaps natural, psychological, or supernatural. Those who are able to uncover these hidden meanings are known as diviners and this might be a shaman, priest, or another type of holy person. It can also be a witch. A diviner is a person we turn to when we want to understand more about the mysteries of life.

Divination can be of three main varieties—inductive, interpretive and intuitive. We will take a closer look at the difference so that we are better able to see the role of tarot in divination.

Inductive Divination

Looking to the skies and nature for our answers is what's known as inductive divination. Astrology has a long history in many religions and cultures from the Mayans to the Chinese and even among Westerners. Diviners are able to see messages in the weather; lightning is seen as messages from the gods; clouds are interpreted as "castles in the air" for those celestial beings in Hinduism. Even the migrational patterns of birds can tell people more about the cycles of time and what the future may hold.

Interpretive Divination

In this method, the diviner will receive information through physical means and then extract meaning from this. These events are manipulated and often subject to interpretation. Two examples would be pyromancy (using fire for divination) and hydromancy (using water for divination). With fire, one may see messages in flames, or throw objects into the fire so the diviner can interpret the reactions. Reading tea leaves is considered interpretive divination.

Intuitive Divination

This is what some refer to as a sixth sense. The person receives information via the senses or they will react to stimuli. Those whose intuition is highly developed are often referred to as psychics or mediums. Necromancy is the ability to talk to the dead because of this sixth-sense.

Divination by intuition is highly energised and could be interpreted as messages from the gods or spirits.

If you think about the ability to read tarot cards, you will need a combination of interpretive divination (understanding a message from a physical object) and intuitive divination (a well-developed sixth sense). You may see tarot readers with other objects, but quite often this is just for show. The two things that you really need are your intuition and your deck of tarot cards. That being said, there is one other key thing we need for divination—an oracle.

THE ROLE OF AN ORACLE IN DIVINATION

Many would find a more delicate way to say this, but an oracle is like the middleman or the vehicle for the message. There are so many examples that we can see. When a fortune teller sees a message through a crystal ball, the crystal ball is the oracle. It can also be a person who receives a message for another person, perhaps from the spirit of a loved one who has passed away. Other examples can include oracle bone—pieces of ox scapula—historically used by the Chinese.

If we focus on an oracle being a person, it is someone who can remain true to themselves and their origins. They have an immense amount of healing energy that can be used in their own lives and to help others. They are able to communicate with plants and animals, not necessarily in a language the average person can understand, but in a way to successfully interpret the message.

So where do tarot cards come into this? Well, tarot can be regarded as an oracle, as an object that transmits messages from the divine (or the universe, depending on your understanding) to the earthly. However, for those who master tarot reading, they can also use this oracle to become an oracle themselves, to interpret the symbols and messages to make better choices in life.

Bear with me as I go over the background and history of tarot. I know that some people are just aching to get straight into their first reading, but others like to gain a complete understanding, often because it improves a person's understanding and therefore confidence. I promise it will be worth the short wait.

WHAT ARE SOME OTHER METHODS OF DIVINATION?

Imagine all of the different cultures over time and how each culture and even era may have had their own interpretations of divination. There is no one way that will work for everyone and once you start appreciating the benefits of tarot readings, you might want to take a closer look at one or more of the following methods of divination.

Celtic Ogham

This is a popular method for Celtic pagans and Wiccans and comes from Ogma/Ogmos, the Celtic god of eloquence and literacy. There are twenty-five sticks, each with a symbol etched into it representing a letter or sound from the Ogham alphabet.

Norse Runes

The runes were considered a gift from Odin, a Norse god and are an ancient alphabet used in Germanic and Scandinavian countries. They are often used by people who have a specific question that relates to a present situation. Runes have no history on paper, but there are numerous carvings of the alphabet in stone, which is why you will find sets made of stone. Germanic tradition has them made of wood.

Tea leaves

Before the seventeenth century, fortune tellers would use the patterns of lead or wax splatter as the oracle. When tea was introduced to Europe, the older methods were replaced with tea leaf reading, officially known as tasseomancy or tasseography. You might want to start with a special cup and saucer that has symbols marked to help with the reading, and there are certain teas that are considered to be better. Stick to Earl Grey or other teas with larger leaves.

Pendulums

If you have ever been pregnant, you may have heard of hanging a crystal or stone on a piece of string to create a pendulum and seeing which way it spins above your belly, which is supposed to determine the sex of the baby. Pendulums are probably one of the easiest methods of divination, because the querent (the person asking the questions) only needs to focus on yes/no questions.

Bones

Osteomancy is the study of bones to find divine messages, as we saw with the Chinese using ox scapula as an oracle. You will often see bones mixed with other objects, like coins or feathers. This is a personal choice for a divination method. Not everyone is comfortable handling animal bones and it's not always easy to find them. Still, the practice has survived for centuries and there has to be a good reason for this.

Numerology

In Modern Paganism, numbers can have amazing spiritual significance and magical meanings. Again, whether you choose to believe in lucky or unlucky numbers is up to you, but there are multiple superstitions throughout history related to the number thirteen. Numbers are also closely related to the planets and astrology.

Palm Reading

There was another phase back in school when we practiced something that really does give divination a bad name... Overnight, we all became palm readers, just because we could spot one line on our palm and decide if it was long or short and then determine if we would live a long life or not! Needless to say, palmistry is more complex than that and can be used to better understand personalities and what may happen in the future.

HOW ARE TAROT CARDS USED FOR DIVINATION?

First of all, let's clear up this idea of tarot cards being a pile of hocus pocus. A lot of my research has been into the fake tarot card readers, as more often than not, this is where the hocus pocus imagery comes in. I've been inside dark rooms that needed curtains, wind chimes, and crystals spread all across the room, and the most bizarre smells that I am too scared to describe. It's that typical sort of image you see on the TV and although some people may use other tools to enhance their intuition, it is not necessary. All you really need is a deck of cards.

Each of the seventy-eight cards has symbols, signs, images, colours, and together with the reader's intuition, the reader is able to use the cards as a guide to understanding likely outcomes. Sometimes, the message is clear, and other times we need to focus a little more to extract the right message. There are some cards that are easy to misinterpret because of their name or harsh images, Death being the perfect example. Pulling the Death card doesn't mean you are facing an early death, which is why it is important to take the time to fully understand the meaning of each card.

A deck of tarot cards is divided into Major Arcana and Minor Arcana. There are twenty-two Major Arcana cards and fifty-six Minor Arcana cards. We are only warming up to the tarots at the moment, so we will just take a brief look at the meanings of each. In Part 2, I want to really get into the symbolic meaning of each card. For now, let's understand the story behind the cards, starting with the Major Arcana cards.

Of the twenty-two Major Arcana cards, all but one are numbered. The first card is the Fool, which has no number, and the following cards are numbered from one to twenty-one. It is the Fool who is the lead character of our story. The other cards represent stages of his journey through life and the significant lessons he learns.

If your tarot reading contains a Major Arcana card, it points to some life lessons that you need to reflect on. If the spread has a large number of Major Arcana cards, the life-changing experiences you are going through are going to have an impact long into the future.

It is worth pointing out that a tarot card can be drawn in an upright position, or reversed (upside down). Again, in Part 2, I will talk about the specific meanings of each card when reversed, but for now, please bear in mind that a reversed tarot doesn't mean the opposite of the upright meaning. The Major Arcana cards being reversed suggest that you aren't paying attention to those life lessons that the world is trying to teach you.

So, we start with the Fool. This card doesn't imply that you are stupid. It points to innocence and new beginnings. This free spirit is ready to take his first steps into the world. Here are the characters he meets on his journey and a brief meaning:

I- The Magician- The Magician has power, but he is also resourceful. He puts on a show and he inspires action.

II- The High Priestess- Her divine feminism represents intuition and sacred knowledge. This card highlights our subconscious mind.

III- The Empress- Another card of great femininity, the Empress is nurturing and reflects nature. She is a sign of beauty and abundance.

IV- The Emperor- He is a figure of authority and often represents a father figure. This card is a sign of establishment. We see the need for structure when the Emperor is drawn.

V- The Hierophant- The Hierophant points to tradition and conformity. He has spiritual and religious wisdom.

VI- The Lovers- Naturally, this card has strong connections to love and harmony, but it also reminds us of our choices and the need to ensure that our values are aligned.

VII- The Chariot- This tarot tells us about our willpower and control. With determination and action, we can find our success.

VIII- Strength- The woman is accompanied by a lion, a symbol of strength and courage. We also appreciate our compassion and the influence that we have on others.

IX- The Hermit- While spending time alone, the Hermit takes time for self-reflection and searching the soul for inner guidance.

X- Wheel of Fortune- It is a positive card, a symbol of good luck and destiny. The wheel also looks at life cycles and karma. It can be a turning point in your life.

XI- Justice- She teaches us about the truth and fairness, often regarding the law. But she also has lessons on cause and effect.

XII- The Hanged Man- The man hanging upside down from a tree points to a pause, a pause so that we can consider new perspectives and let go of things that are holding us back.

XIII- Death - Despite the powerful imagery, we don't have to fear this tarot as much as the name implies. Death represents the end of something, or changes and transformations.

XIV- Temperance- Temperance shows us the importance of patience, balance and our purpose in life.

XV- The Devil- The Devil highlights our attachments and even addictions. This card also explores our sexuality and some of the things that restrict us.

XVI- The Tower- There are sudden changes when the Tower is drawn and this can create chaos and disruption. However, there will be a revelation that will help you continue your journey.

XVII- The Star- The Star is a sign of hope and faith. There is an element of spirituality and renewal as we find our purpose again.

XVIII- The Moon- There might be a reason to be anxious or fearful. This card is also related to illusion, our subconscious and our instincts.

XIX- The Sun- The Sun is a fun card that fills us with warmth and positivity. We can appreciate its vitality and can point to success.

XX- Judgement- Judgement shows us the need to forgive. It also represents rebirth and an inner calling.

XXI- The World- The last of the Major Arcana cards points to the completion of the journey and an accomplishment. It also represents travel and integration.

Obviously, there is a lot more to each card. If it were that easy, we would all be reading tarot cards, but this is a good summary to give you an overall picture. Next, let's take a look at how the Minor Arcana cards are organised.

The Minor Arcana tarots are divided into four suits—Wands, Swords, Cups, and Pentacles (sometimes referred to as Coins). There are ten numbered cards in each suit and four court cards—the Page, Knight, Queen and King.

The Wands Suit

The Wands are associated with the element of fire. They are symbols of passion, determination and inspiration, which arc three themes that you will see throughout the journey of this suit. The Wands are energetic cards and encourage action and the creation of new plans. Here are a few words that will give you an idea of the meaning of each of the Wands:

Ace of Wands- Willpower, desires, creation

Two of Wands- Leaving home, decision making, planning

Three of Wands- Looking forward, growth

Four of Wands- Home, a sense of community, festivities

Five of Wands- Discussions, competitiveness, rivals

Six of Wands- Triumph, success, public recognition

Seven of Wands- Perseverance, keeping control, safeguarding

Eight of Wands- Fast decisions and action, momentum

Nine of Wands- Strength, hardiness, durability

Ten of Wands- Success, a heavy burden, responsibilities

Page of Wands- Liberty, discovery, joy

Knight of Wands- Bravery, movement, adventure

Queen of Wands- Courage, happiness, determination

Kings of Wands- The bigger picture, conquering obstacles, a leader

The Cups Suit

The Cups are linked to the element of water and are linked to our feelings, our intuition and our creativity. Often, the Cups will explain things about our relationships, be they romantic, partnerships, or friendships. They will also provide insight into our imagination and inner voice.

Ace of Cups- New emotions, intuition, spiritualism

Two of Cups- Coming together, connections, partnership

Three of Cups- The community, joy, friendships

Four of Cups- Indifference, observation, a lack of connection

Five of Cups- Loss and grief, defeatism

Six of Cups- Fond memories, familiarity, recuperation

Seven of Cups- Decisions, looking for your purpose, daydreams

Eight of Cups- A rude awakening, walking away and leaving things in the past

Nine of Cups- Gratification, stability within your emotions, splendour

Ten of Cups- Internal joy, self-realization, wishes becoming a reality

Page of Cups- Pleasant surprises, idealism, sensitivity

Knight of Cups- A romantic, listening to your heart's desires

Queen of Cups- Understanding, tranquility, comfort

King of Cups- Compassion, control, equilibrium

The Swords Suit

The element of air is linked to the Swords Suit and it reflects our intelligence, reason, and truth. This suit also helps us to better understand communication and conflicts that arise. We all have the ability to use the power of our intellect, but at the same time, the swords are double-edged, so we have to be careful about how we use this power.

Ace of Swords- A sharp mind, clear thinking, developments

Two of Swords- Tough decisions and indecision, impasse

Three of Swords- Broken hearts, pain, grief

Four of Swords- Taking a break, mending, scrutiny

Five of Swords- Uncontrolled ambition, cunning, the need to win no matter what

Six of Swords- Change, moving forward, leaving things behind you

Seven of Swords- Deceit, dishonesty, scheming

Eight of Swords- Self-victimising, restrictions, confinement

Nine of Swords- Trauma, stress and anxiety, despondency

Ten of Swords- Fiasco, disappointment, collapse

Page of Swords- Intrigue, energetic mind, restlessness

Knight of Swords- Standing up for your beliefs, action, haste

Queen of Swords- Intricacy, mental clarity, perception

King of Swords- Self-control, head over the heart

The Pentacles Suit

As the Pentacles are also known as the Coins; there is a theme here of finance, business and career and this suit often points to things in the long-term future. The Pentacles are associated with the element of earth and so this suit also informs us of our stability and health, even our feelings of sensuality.

Ace of Pentacles- New ventures and opportunities, wealth

Two of Pentacles- Weighing your options, prioritising, adapting to change.

Three of Pentacles- Working together, creation, team efforts

Four of Pentacles- Preservation, thriftiness, security

Five of Pentacles- Necessities, insecurity, financial hardship

Six of Pentacles- Charity, sharing, giving

Seven of Pentacles- Hard work and attention to detail, perseverance

Eight of Pentacles- Enthusiasm, high expectations, apprenticeship

Nine of Pentacles- Reap the benefits of your hard work, luxury, rewards

Ten of Pentacles- Birthright, inheritance, collecting

Page of Pentacles- Drive, hard work, passion

Knight of Pentacles- Diligence, responsibility, efficiency

Queen of Pentacles- Comfort, financial security, possibility

King of Pentacles- Plenty, wealth, stability

This is barely scratching the surface of the seventy-eight tarot cards: it's like peeling back just one fraction of a corner and you can probably understand now why it can take years to fully master the art of tarot reading. As I said, there is no need for you to start memorising each of the short descriptions I have given. In Part 2, we will describe the images and symbols of each card so that it becomes easier to appreciate the messages, both upright and reversed.

CHOOSING THE RIGHT TAROT DECK FOR YOU

This is such a crazy question and I can only relate it to choosing crystals for healing. You have so many options and people will recommend different ones, but with so many different tarot card decks, it can be difficult to know which one is going to be right for you.

To name a few examples, there are tarot decks for witches, Gothic tarot decks, Renaissance decks, mermaid, fairy tale, mystical, Manga, and I kid you not, I have even seen an Edgar Allan Poe tarot set. There are large-sized cards, mini sets, traditional and modern. The number one rule, like in many areas of divination and spiritualism, is that you have to choose a tarot deck that you have a connection with. There was (and some still believe) a superstition that you should never buy your own tarot cards and that someone should give them to you. Many people, me included, prefer to choose their own deck to make sure it has meaning to them. For example, each different style will have different image designs and it's important that these images tap into your intuition. If you can, look at every card in the deck. I've seen a few that have amazing Major Arcanas but the Minor Arcanas leave a lot to be desired, and vice versa.

The size and quality of the deck are also worth considering. My family laughs at my tiddly hands and a large tarot deck looks completely out of place, plus I don't feel comfortable with them. Personally, I like decks that are a similar size to a standard deck of cards.

My final bit of advice for finding the right deck is to go for quality, because it will be worth the extra investment. Because of the time it takes to learn the different tarot meanings, it makes more sense to buy a deck that will stay with you for years. Once you gain confidence with your go-to deck, you can start adding to your collection.

Despite so many options, for the sake of this book, I am going to stick to my first deck, the Rider Waite tarot set. I fell in love with the colours, and the imagery and symbols in these cards were real eye-openers for me.

I'm sure you are still keen to dive straight into your readings, but in the next chapter, we are going to take a more specific look at what tarot is good for, beyond making predictions of the future.

2

WHAT IS TAROT GOOD FOR?

Because many of us have been given the wrong impression about tarot, it's easy to understand why we might assume it's just a method for fortune-telling. The next logical assumption from here is that the future is unpredictable and therefore, tarot readers are just out to earn a quick buck.

As I was exploring the sad world of psychic scammers, I came across a perfect example of why non-believers feel that tarot is not good for anything. I signed up for a free online tarot reading just this year. This was not because I wasn't confident in my own capabilities, but more out of curiosity. I was dealt my three cards and the first one said, "You are in for a difficult and unpredictable year", but if I wanted to find out more, I would have to register with the site. Well, first of all, we are in the midst of a global pandemic right now so it is unlikely that anyone will disagree with this statement. Second, this tarot reading was probably not good for anything, because I didn't want to be bombarded with further emails from them.

You might find it weird why such a dedicated tarot reader would discuss this rather negative side to tarot, but it is only fair that you appreciate that I am able to see things from the point of view of the believer and the non-believer. I have had readings which have literally been no good and others that have surprised me beyond belief. Just remember, that when you hire a contractor for your home or try a new hairdresser, even a restaurant, the same thing can happen. We can be amazed or disappointed by our experiences, but it's not to say that every provider follows the same ethics and standards.

Knowing that tarot cards can bring about a wealth of good made me more determined to learn the art myself, so that I knew I would be getting the most amount of benefit from the cards.

As I briefly mentioned, tarot cards can be used to gain a greater understanding of the bigger questions in our lives. We can use them to help us make decisions regarding love and romance, our education and careers, as well as our health (both mental and physical). The cards can convey advice about travel, moving home, or even a change in country. Used in the right way, tarot cards can offer spiritual guidance that helps us learn more about who we really are and what we want to achieve in life.

Regardless of why you want to explore this form of occult reading, I am going to ask one thing of you. From here on in, try to have an open mind and after reading this chapter, I hope you can appreciate the full range of benefits that the cards can offer and not just see them as a way of telling you what lies ahead. A very wise spiritualist once told me that the psychic practices are there to light our path and help us to see through the mist and the darkness; they aren't there to determine our path. If you think of tarot in this way, it can be compared to asking for help from an online recipe; the chef isn't going to make the dish for you.

TAROT CARDS AND THE TRACKING OF PERSONAL INFORMATION

Though it feels like I am always trying to defend certain practises, there is a method to my madness. So many techniques in life are portrayed by society in a certain way that it can put us off even before we have begun to consider the possibilities. Journaling is another one of these techniques. Some may see it as something young teenage girls do just to write about their latest crush. As someone who started their first journal at around that age, I can confirm that this is true, but as the years went on, my journal became my own therapeutic retreat.

Let's start out with a fact to get us all a little more intrigued. A study published online by Cambridge University Press showed that those people who wrote about a traumatic, stressful, or emotional event for fifteen to twenty minutes on three to five occasions had significantly better physical and psychological outcomes than those who didn't. It was the psychologist, James Pennebaker, who carried out the extensive studies on journaling and its benefits, one of which was that those who had participated in the study and wrote about the things they would never dream of telling anyone else had fewer medical appointments in the following months.

The language of the journal entries changed over time. "I" statements were often replaced with "he" or "she", which suggests that the writers were beginning to see things from different perspectives, considering how others think and feel. There were also more "because" statements, suggesting better reasoning of situations. Journaling is an effective way to heal both the old wounds that you thought you had laid to rest and the more recent ones that still sting.

Before looking at the relationship between tarot readings and journaling, here are a few other reasons for writing down your emotions:

- Writing improves your language learning and encourages you to expand your vocabulary, improving your **verbal intelligence**.
- Journaling lets you explore your emotions and those of others. It enhances **self-awareness** and therefore your emotional intelligence.
- Working on both your IQ and EQ will have a

positive effect on your verbal **communication skills**.
- When writing in a journal, even when writing about the past and the future, it helps you to pull yourself back to the present and concentrate on how you feel in that moment, a great tool for **mindfulness**.
- Writing recomposes our thoughts and ideas and can help to boost the **memory**.
- When you include your **goals** in your journal, they become more real and important once on paper, like you have committed to them, and so you become more determined to achieve them.
- At first, you may feel like you don't have anything to write about. You will be surprised by how much **creativity** you have once you actually start writing, not because it is forced, but because when you open the 'Pandora's box of feelings', they will flow.
- You will start to **heal**. Getting all of this weight off your chest and onto paper is such an immense relief and you can start to see the positive in things, even if it is just small steps.
- When you learn how to write about both the good and the bad, your confidence begins to grow, especially when you spend some time journaling about your achievements.

For me personally, I found journaling and tarots to be the perfect combination for three reasons. First, they helped me to improve my self-discipline. Before, despite knowing that journaling was helping me mentally, I would only pick it up once in a while, maybe even only once every few months. Second, tarot reading helped me to explore new ideas, each new image would give me something fresh to contemplate or remind me of a past experience that I felt I should understand better. And so, third, I started to write more frequently, including it as one of my healthy habits.

Reflecting on my feelings and becoming more aware of my inner self was a great help for taking the images and symbols of the cards and deciphering how they related to my personal journal and my destiny. At the same time, these striking images helped me to see the role of other people in my life and to see problems from a different angle. Instead of there only being one solution, tarots allowed me to see alternative routes to achieving my objective, and more often than not, in ways more practical than I would have thought of without the help of the cards. Between the tarots and journaling, I learnt that the easy road wouldn't necessarily reap the greatest rewards, but the two tools showed me the best way to face the more challenging road and the greater rewards.

Of course, there are still other ways that you can explore your creativity with the help of tarots. I know an amazing artist who will draw and paint her interpretations of a reading. Her work is fascinating, because although I recognise certain elements of the card, I can see how the final result is truly unique to her. If I had drawn the same cards in a reading, I probably would have a completely different interpretation, but that's the beauty of tarot.

TAROT AND PSYCHOTHERAPY

It may surprise you to learn that divination and science have not always been on opposite sides of the court. Carl Jung was one of the most respected psychiatrists and psychoanalysts of the twentieth century. Aside from his extensive work as the founder of analytical psychology, Jung was also interested in spiritualism and the paranormal and occult. Jung felt that tarot cards had potential as a tool in psychology for unlocking the unconscious mind.

In a 1933 seminar, Jung said:

"These cards… are psychological images, symbols with which one plays, as the unconscious seems to play with its contents. They combine in certain ways, and the different combinations correspond to the playful development of events in the history of mankind…

For example, the symbol of the sun, or the symbol of the man hung up by the feet, or the tower struck by lightning, or the wheel of fortune, and so on. Those are sort of archetypal ideas, of a differentiated nature, which mingle with the ordinary constituents of the flow of the unconscious, and therefore it is applicable for an intuitive method that has the purpose of understanding the flow of life, possibly even predicting future events, at all events lending itself to the reading of the conditions of the present moment."

By learning how the present has evolved from the past, he felt that it was possible to make intuitive predictions on the future. Just as many of Jung's theories were contentious, not everyone would agree with the use of tarot cards for psychology, but there are many who followed his work and you will still find some of his followers today using tarot cards to encourage clients to better understand aspects of their lives.

But why is this? They are visual images and visual images are frequently used in psychology to discover underlying thoughts or feelings as well as those thoughts that we find more difficult to express. How many times have you got into a pickle because you haven't found the right words for a certain situation? You know your boss wouldn't look at you with that weird look if you could just present your findings in a PowerPoint. Sometimes a little note from your partner with a smiley face and a heart means more than the words "I love you".

Tarot cards can be used as a tool, just like psychologists would use the Rorschach Test or the Thematic Apperception Test. You have probably seen the Rorschach Test in films—

this set of ink blogs are shown to patients to understand a person's perceptions better. The Thematic Apperception Test uses a set of images that the patient/client uses to tell a story, again, highlighting certain aspects of the person's personality, beliefs, and inner conflicts.

Visual images are crucial in psychology because, in layman's terms, they help us to find our words. In the situations where we know what is troubling us, a tarot card can spark a light that jogs our brain into focusing on what we are thinking and how we are feeling. These images can essentially remind the brain of what we are feeling or even what we want to say.

Take, for example, a person who is overwhelmed with life, there is so much going on that everything is bundled together and they can't make sense of it. There are people ready to help them, but at this point, they don't even know what they want or need. If you show this person an image of nature, a green forest untouched by humans, their mind immediately understands peace. An image of waves gently rolling onto the shore instils a sense of calm. The person knows that they need a break, but either of the images specifies that they need to find some tranquility in their life and, quite probably, some time alone. I can only testify to this, because this is how I have felt in the same situation, looking at the same images and when talking to others in need of help who have felt the same way.

If we take this one step further, it doesn't matter if you are the boss or the employee, the parent or the child, there are times when we know what we need, but we struggle to verbalise this, for fear that we will upset the other party.

Tarot cards provide a comfortable way to express how we feel.

For me, this is far more relevant with tarot cards than with the Rorschach Test and the Thematic Test. Don't get me wrong, I have also appreciated the benefits of these tests, but with the help of professionals. With tarot cards, I was able to experience similar benefits without studying for a career in psychology. I know a lot of people who were too shy to talk about their deepest feelings with a psychologist and even more who were just embarrassed. The cards help to unravel these feelings by yourself, which is incredibly empowering.

Tarot cards are a massive help when people are stuck. I hate to make assumptions, but it's very possible that you are reading this book because you are 'stuck' in life. Even non-believers can relate to moments in life when they don't have the answer. When you get the point where you can't see the solution, tarot cards can zone in on the areas that you are having problems with. The cards that you draw can give a new, refreshing perspective that you may not have thought about before.

TAROT AND THE CHAKRAS

For further benefits from the cards, it is worth understanding how they correlate with our chakras. We have seven chakras starting at the base of the spine and going up to the crown of our head. These spinning energy wheels can help you connect with the energy of the cards. Here's how:

The Element of Spirit

The Major Arcana, as the cards that teach us the bigger lessons in life, are the most spiritual. Psychoanalysts influenced by Jung believe that our unconscious contains a number of archetypes, which is where we get our insights from. The Crown Chakra is also related to life's lessons, while the Third Eye Chakra sparks our intuition so that we are better able to understand the spiritual information we receive.

The Element of Air

The Swords suit is linked to the element of air and it focuses on creating ideas and thoughts and then how we communicate these creations. Considering the position of the Throat Chakra, you can see how it enables us to improve our communication and to speak the truth.

The Element of Water

The Cups is a water suit. Water is a sign of our emotions, love and the relationships we have. The world depends on water as much as we depend on our hearts. The Heart Chakra is obviously tied to love and other powerful emotions we feel.

The Element of Fire

The Solar Plexus Chakra and the Sacral Chakra are located in the lower part of your back. They are associated with action and fertility, respectively. The internal power that we have, our passion for life and our pleasures, burn like a fire inside us. The Wands suit is also about fertility.

The Element of Earth

At the base of our spines, you will find the Root Chakra and as you can imagine, it is what keeps us grounded. We relate this chakra to our survival instincts and the material things that we need in life—food, shelter, etc. It makes sense that the Pentacles, associated with the earth element, is also linked to the Root Chakra.

I find that it helps if you meditate with your tarot deck, especially as you concentrate on the energy that flows up throughout your body. Your chakras will absorb the energy of the cards, making connections between the suits, the elements, and the messages that you are being shown.

TAROT AND WITCHCRAFT

As we have seen, there are competing ideas about the power of tarot and where its claimed insights originate. Some view tarot and/or the reader as an oracle, acting as a conduit for knowledge from the divine or from the universe at large. Others, like Jung, view tarot as symbolic tools to uncover what is hiding in our own unconscious minds. There are also some who believe that each card has a special power and a magic ability behind it. The great thing, in this understanding, is that we can unlock this magic without actively knowing so. Tarot spellcasting is a way of using creative visualisation, with the help of images and symbols in cards, to develop powerful intentions. The idea is that certain cards will help you with these intentions, depending on what it exactly is that you desire. Remember that the suits can be used for certain benefits: the Swords will help with your way of thinking, the Wands tap into your creativity, the Pentacles are related to wealth and wellbeing, and the Cups are for emotions. Let's look at some of the Major Arcana cards and their purported magical uses.

The Magician- a logical place to start, the Magician channels energy with his wand and directs it with his pointing finger. You can cast a spell to ask the Magician to protect you.

The Star- you can use the star to receive good things, gifts and blessings. You can cast a spell to help you open up and be prepared for what you are asking of the universe.

Death- Death is an amazing card for tarot spellcasting. It can bring an end to all kinds of things, so that you can make way for new, brighter things. You can cast a spell to put an end to bad habits or relationships that you want to say goodbye to.

Wheel of Fortune- a wheel constantly turns, like the planets moving in our solar system. If you are frustrated that things aren't moving quickly enough for you, you can use the energy of the Wheel of Fortune to get the movement you wish.

If you are looking for more good reasons to use the tarot cards, witchcraft and tarot spells are the perfect examples. There is an infinite number of spells that you can cast and this doesn't necessarily have to be for your own good. These powerful intentions can also be used for the good of others. Naturally, if you are suffering or struggling, you will first want to concentrate on your own healing, but when you start feeling stronger, look for ways that you can use tarots and spells to help people in your life.

The main takeaway is that when you learn how to read tarot cards correctly, you will be able to unlock an immense amount of information about your life, the past and the future. You will be able to see things with so much more clarity that it becomes easier to make the more difficult decisions in life. You can see things from new perspectives which opens the door to a world of new opportunities.

Because of this, you can see how tarot readings aren't just a tool for predicting the future. The cards are an invaluable tool that helps someone understand more about what is burning through their minds; they help us to find words when we aren't sure how to express feelings, and they can be used to draw upon the energy in the universe, and even to help others. Before I started my exploration of the cards, I had no idea that there was so much good to be found!

A LITTLE HISTORY OF THE TAROTS

Despite it being decades ago, I remember hating history and having to study dates of things that were going to serve no purpose in my life. When I first got hooked on spiritualism, it was because I was a skeptic and began looking into ways almost to disprove the practices. This is how I actually got excited about history and learning about the origins of tarot cards was just as fascinating.

As we go back through time and understand how the tarots became what they are today, we also get to look at some of the typical myths that surround them, why they came about and how they aren't true.

Uncovering the Egyptian Gods Myth

One of the biggest myths that you will hear is that the tarot cards were written by Egyptian gods. This is because

Antoine Court de Gebelin, a French Freemason, published a rather complete guide of the tarots in 1781. He stated that the symbols of the cards came from secrets of Egyptian priests, which came from the Egyptians gods. Now, nothing of what Gebelin wrote was based on any evidence found. As open-minded as I am, I am not inclined to believe in something without some form of proof. So, let's move on.

Are the Tarot Cards European?

We Westerners have a habit of claiming fame for, or at least popularising, things that were in existence before. We have done the same with things like yoga and chakra healing, both of which have been around for thousands of years. While we aren't as bold as to say that we invented such practises, we still find ways of making just a slight modernisation to call it our own. The same thing happened with tarot.

If you look to the twelfth century, the Chinese played games with strips of bamboo in their hands. Eventually, the bamboo was replaced with round, square, or rectangular paper or papyrus. By the 1300s, these cards had made their way to Egypt. The first concepts of playing cards came from Egypt, but the original idea of a game of cards played in the hands was Chinese.

Tarot decks were first documented in Italy in the mid-fifteenth century. The name of tarot derives from the Italian *tarocchi*, which itself is of uncertain origin. However, in the medieval period, *taroch* was used to mean 'foolishness', and of course we still have the Fool as the tarot protagonist, so this seems a reasonable explanation for the name.

In the sixteenth century, tarot was still seen as a game and one for the wealthy. Needless to say, without printing, the cards were hand-painted and the Italians with money had their own sets of cards painted with images of family members and friends. The Italians used these cards to play a game called 'carte de trionfi', the cards of triumph. A player would be dealt cards and then use the imagery to create a story. In the fifteenth century, the Spanish also started hand painting cards, although the imagery was very similar to that of the Italian, as both were considered the Latin deck. As the Spanish had a great influence on various South American countries, the cards soon made their way to these cultures too. Even in France, in the 14th and 15th century, the cards were used for purely entertainment purposes and not for divination.

It wasn't until the mid-18th century that cards began to gain a mystical reputation and people started using them for divination. At this point, the Queens had been added and the terms Minor and Major Arcana had been established. It is also at this point that things start getting a little controversial. The printing press was well established by this point, so it wasn't only the wealthy that could get their hands on a deck of tarot cards. As the cards became more popular, more theories of their origins and meanings started to arise.

We have already discussed the myth of the Egyptian gods by Court de Gebelin. Other scholars followed the path of Gebelin. Jean-Baptiste Alliette wrote a book on *the Art of Reading Cards* in 1791, and he believed the cards originated with the Book of Thoth, which belonged to the Egyptian god of wisdom. Throughout this period, the cards were seen to be esoteric, only understood by a small group of people, and the game converted into a complex set of images that required special knowledge to fully understand. Alliette and de Gebelin are nonetheless credited with popularising the use of tarot for cartomancy, and Alliette created the first known deck specifically for this purpose.

As the Victorian era came to an end, spiritualism and the occult had reached a new level of popularity with the upper classes. Parties may have been held with palm readings and tea leaf readings, and of course, a deck of tarot cards would be present.

As the tarot has evolved and new variants emerged in symbolism and usage, disagreements have inevitably arisen over what is authentic or correct. People have argued about the court cards, the originals and the various replacements. Then, more recently, we have Jung and his influence on the tarot cards, archetypes and psychology, steering the cards away from religion and more toward psychoanalysis. In the twentieth century, Rabbi Steven Fisdel peeled back all non-Jewish imagery from the cards and was left with a set of cards with numbers and Hebrew letters. This highlighted the link between the tarot and

Kabbalah—the ancient Jewish tradition of mystical readings of the Bible.

While people choose to disagree on certain aspects of the tarots, this is perfectly normal and there are plenty of other things in our world, both scientific and spiritual, that we may not see eye to eye on. Rather than using this to discredit the art and even the magic behind the cards, I decided this was another reason to learn how to read your own cards. The personal interpretations of the cards are what is going to help you understand more about your life. I love history but more out of curiosity and not to prove which scholars are right or wrong. Really, I can see a valid point in a lot of what they have to say.

HOW THE DIFFERENT DECKS DEVELOPED OVER TIME

From the simple images yet the intricate gold design of early cards to the Harry Potter or the witty Silicon Valley tarot, there have been countless adaptations of the tarot cards. It's impossible to mention all of the designs, but here are some of the most significant that have impacted the evolution of the cards.

The Lenormand-style decks from the 1860s were the first to incorporate chromolithography, or multi-colored prints. These decks were a combination of the standard playing deck (hearts, clubs, diamonds, and spades) and fortune-telling images.

Prior to the Lenormand cards, a British company printed a different set of cards that had images and little snippets of advice on the bottom, such as "Be always on your guard; he who easily believes is easily deceived." Though the images aren't like those of the tarot cards, they did come with a booklet of instructions on how to use the cards, much like the Lenormand cards.

Three of the most common tarot decks that we see today are the tarot de Marseille and the tarot of Nouveau, the Rider-Waite-Smith, and the Crowley-Harris Thoth set. It's worth looking into these in a little more depth.

The Tarot de Marseille

Many of today's tarot decks still follow the same pattern of the tarot de Marseille. When the French conquered Italy in 1499, they most likely took the tarot back to France with them and then when it was reintroduced to Italy, it had the Marseille design.

The actual deck has the same structure as other decks, but each suit is known in its French name: Batons- Wands, Épées- Swords Coupes- Cups, and Deniers- Coins. To complete the Minor Arcana cards, there are four face cards, the Valet (Page), the Cavalier/Chevalier (Knight), the Dame (Queen) and the Roi, (King). The main difference you will notice with the Major Arcana cards is the Roman numerals, which are additive (the original system of ancient Rome.

. . .

Tarot Nouveau

The Tarot Nouveau was never intended for divination, which is why the French call this deck the tarot á jouer, or playing tarot. It uses the symbols we see on a standard playing deck (hearts, diamonds, spades and clubs) but the Ace card is numbered 1. Also, instead of the Page, we have the Jack.

Interestingly, the Major Arcana cards have an urban and rural representation. So, taking the first card, which we would see as the Fool, for the urban representation, we see a sad clown, and the rural representation is of a fool and a ballerina. The other significant difference is that the Roman numerals have been replaced with Arabic numerals (digits).

Crowley-Harris Thoth Tarot Deck

Aleister Crowley had the idea of a short project to update the tarot. He worked with Lady Frieda Harris, who painted the deck. The task was more demanding than originally expected, and in the end, it took around six years, finishing in 1943. The images became much more detailed, with symbols of science, philosophy, and the occult. In 1944, Crowley finished writing a book that was intended to be used with the deck.

Only the Queen remained the same out of the court/face cards. The King was changed to the Knight, the traditional Knight became the Prince and the Page was portrayed as the Princess in the Thoth tarot deck. There were also some name changes with Major Arcana cards:

- The Magician- The Magus
- The High Priestess- The Priestess
- Strength- Lust
- Wheel of Fortune- Fortune
- Justice- Adjustment
- Temperance- Art
- Judgement- The Æon*
- The World- The Universe

*According to the religion of the Thelema, which Aleister Crowley founded, history can be separated into aeons and each aeon has a form of magical and religious expression, a key to appreciating Thelemic Magick.

Rider-Waite-Smith Tarot Deck

I have worked with the Rider deck ever since I got the tarot bug, so to speak. For me, it's the deck that is richest in imagery and symbols and it made it easier for me to understand tarot as a whole. It was a combination of the talents of A.E. Waite, the academic who wrote the instructions, and Pamela Colman Smith, who illustrated the cards. They were first published in 1909 by the Rider company.

I won't go too much into the imagery now, because there is a chapter dedicated to this. It's important to know that the

Rider-Waite-Smith (hereon known as the Rider deck) doesn't have such a strong Christian meaning, which makes it that more universal. For example, the Pope in the Rider deck is called the Hierophant. Smith also added much more imagery to the Minor Arcanas and Waite made some changes so that the Major Arcana cards had a stronger correlation with astrology. He put Strength before Justice so that Strength was linked to Leo and Justice to Libra. He removed one of the Lovers to tie in with Gemini.

Theme-Based Tarot Cards

Whether we like it or not, everything has the ability to become commercialised. I think to some extent, the commercialisation of tarot cards has not been a bad thing. As tarot has entered the modern world, the different decks available today make it more appealing to the many. You now have the option to select a deck of tarot cards that reflects your personality or your hobby.

If you are interested in healing, you may like the deck that is aimed at herbs and their healing abilities. If you want to explore the supernatural, you have a Ghosts and Spirits Deck.

The Modern Witch tarot has images of women of all races, shapes and sizes as the main figures in the cards. You will like this modern twist as it has a funky biker on her 'chariot' and the Emperor has a nice power trouser suit; even the Hermit appears to be closing her laptop.

For the male readers, don't worry, there are also decks that have been designed with you in mind. The Everyman tarot is based on the Rider deck, but cleverly depicts how a modern man copes with the experiences of today's world.

BUSTING THE TAROT MYTHS

If I have done my job correctly, you will hopefully know that tarot cards do not require a dark room with a crystal ball and a crystal layout around you. You also don't need to pay a fortune, have a degree in psychology or be a practising witch. Now that you know tarot is about using your intuition, you also know that you don't need to be a psychic.

Another typical myth I have heard so often is that tarot is evil or dangerous. Throughout history, man has been gifted with intelligence. People have used this for good and for evil. Tarot cards can be used for evil, but this comes down to your intention, not the cards. The cards themselves are neither evil nor dangerous. This myth may have come about because when people see certain aspects of their unconscious, it can scare them. But, it's not really fair to blame our unconscious or our fears on tarot.

I know I have touched on this but I just want to remind everyone again, not because you weren't paying attention, but because it is such a widely believed myth that it's worth reiterating. The cards are not predicting your future. They can be used to see what might happen if you continue on the path that you are on. That being said, you have the ability to make any changes you want. The guidance the cards offer you can provide hope, but they were never intended to be a tool to fix you.

Life is funny sometimes! I consider myself to be extremely confident at tarot readings, I would even go to call myself an expert, but I feel too big-headed. That being said, I recognise that there are lots of different approaches to, and interpretations of, tarot and I am only proficient in one particular tradition. The scholars over the last centuries have all had their interpretations, some based on opinion, others on fact. It's still been a great trip through time to understand some of the most significant moments of the tarot cards.

Now that we have looked at what the tarots are not, it's time to gain more insight as to what a reading looks like from start to finish.

4

A TAROT READING

There are so many different settings for a tarot reading. I have been in little rooms in the back of a holistic shop, in my own home, in the psychic's home, in a field at a festival, in a shopping center, you name it, I have tried it. It's easy to blame the tarot reader for hearing something that we don't want to, or for not finding the answers we were hoping to, but the setting has a very key role in the reading. If you go for a massage, would you prefer to be in the middle of a field in a rock concert or in a beauty parlour? You wouldn't ask your doctor for your blood test results in the middle of a supermarket, and so on.

When getting the right setting, I always run through a checklist of my four spaces, the physical, mental, emotional, and spiritual. Let's touch a little on each of these.

- **Your physical, safe space**

Basically, this is everything in your setting that you can touch, from the comfort of your seating to the texture of your table, or the tarot cloth you lay down. Some people like candles and crystals and I admit that I will also use them on occasions, but only when the mood takes me. Sometimes, all I feel the need for is my deck, sometimes I like to sit in the garden, other times on the living room floor. Your physical space has to be the right balance between comfort and privacy. You will need some privacy so that you feel in a safe place where you will not be interrupted.

- **A calm mental space**

Clarity and focus are the goals here, but we all know that this is a challenge. Busy lives tend to occupy our minds and it's hard to put aside the list of things we have to do. It's a great idea to start with a short meditation or even some deep breathing to start to clear the mind. You will notice that knowing exactly what your questions are will help to slow down your racing mind and get more out of your reading. Another thing to remember is that some people like having the herbs, candles, crystals, etc., while for others, this feels like clutter and a cluttered physical space can lead to a cluttered mind.

- **A peaceful emotional space**

As well as feeling safe prior to your reading, you also want to ensure that you are feeling positive and that your emotional baggage is left behind. Negative emotions could cause you to read the cards in the wrong way, possibly even to see things that aren't there. As you use deep breathing for your mental space, exhale the negativity and inhale the positivity.

- **An intuitive spiritual space**

The spiritual space is what will allow you to tap into the energy of the universe and of the cards. Making sure your chakras are balanced is a good start for boosting your energy and creating a stronger connection with your spiritual self. If you are looking for an alternative to meditation, you could use mantras or affirmations to increase your confidence and the faith in your own intuition.

One of my more amusing errors early on was dedicating too much time to the physical space and not enough on the mental, emotional, and spiritual. My spare room was converted into the perfect image of a supernatural den. The colour scheme was spot on, the enchanting smells filled the room, my meditation CD was playing and there were more candles than in Ikea. I found it bizarre in those first few weeks that there seemed to be an energy wall around me that prevented me gaining the necessary spiritual connection. That's when I dialed it right back and focused more on preparing myself and not my environment.

As with anything new in life, don't worry if you don't feel that you have the right space straight away, because it might take a few sessions before you decide what feels comfortable for and what doesn't. It's not like making a mistake will harm you. It's about finding that perfect space for you so that your intuition is enhanced and your reading is clearer. Your attitude, however, is something that you should get right from the outset.

HAVING THE RIGHT ATTITUDE AND INTENTIONS FOR YOUR TAROT READING

It sounds a little harsh, but if you just want to know what is going to happen in your future, you might be better off having someone read your tarots for you. This is only because it takes quite a bit of time and dedication to learning about tarot cards and the result is far more than simply fortune-telling.

Your intentions should be to find a greater level of truth regarding your life, more guidance, and direction. The cards are a tool that should be used for personal growth and to learn more about yourself and your role in the universe. Imagine the cards as a bridge from your physical being to your spiritual self.

Like any divination tool, the tarot cards mustn't be used to control your life's decisions. Instead, they are to help you provide wisdom and insights on things that you already have information on. Let's say your question is whether or not you should go for the promotion that is available at work. If the cards indicate that the new role will require more hours at work, it's a sign that you shouldn't take it. It indicates that you need to consider if you have available time, if you can free up additional time for your hobbies and whether or not there is enough compensation for these extra hours. If you take the job because "the cards told you", you have the wrong attitude about the practice. You have to take responsibility for your own life and your actions.

You also need to remain objective at all times. A negative attitude will more than likely lead to an unsatisfactory reading. If you have a question, but you have already made your mind up about what you think the answer or solution is, then your reading will be biased.

One thing that many aren't aware of is the importance of urgency. If there is a movie on TV this weekend and you have wanted to watch it for absolutely ever, you are more likely to sit down and watch it. If the movie is 50/50, there will be something more interesting to do. If the answer to your question is urgent, you will find that the insights you read are more direct, clearer, and conclusive.

I promise you, the more readings that you do, the more confident you will be with your readings. This continuous effort drives your intuition to new levels and over time, you start to see more about your interpretations. Like an athlete pushing themselves to the next level, your rewards will surprise you and encourage you to learn even more about your inner self.

THE ART OF FORMING YOUR QUESTIONS

A genie appears in front of you and instead of three wishes, you can ask three questions. Would you know which questions to ask? If the same genie appeared on a Sunday morning or one month before Christmas, would those questions be the same? Sometimes, planning your questions can be trickier than the actual reading, mainly because you can't change your mind halfway through the reading or things just won't make sense. First, let's look at the different types of questions that you can ask:

- Questions about the present
- Questions about the past
- Questions about the future
- Questions about making decisions
- Open-ended questions
- Yes/no questions- bear in mind that this type of question won't lead to a direct yes or no, because the answers aren't always quite as simple. When you learn more about the specific symbols on the cards, you will be more prepared to understand complexities and find your yes/no answer.

Here is a guide to formulating the perfect tarot questions:

1. **Begin with open-ended questions.**

Questions that start with who, what, where, why, how will give you a chance to explore the options available to make a change in particular situations. Questions like "How can

I get out of my financial difficulties?" allow for a more in-depth analysis of the card's meanings.

2. Steer clear of questions that shift the responsibility

As I mentioned before, tarot cards are to provide meaning, not to tell you what choices to make. Questions that start with 'should', 'will' or 'when' tend to move that responsibility to the cards. If you take the same question as above, but asked "When will I get out of financial difficulties?" the cards might show you a sign. If you haven't resolved your problems by then, you may end up wrongly blaming the cards.

3. Discover more about your general life direction

If you don't have a particular question, you can still carry out a reading to learn more about the path you are on right now or about the energies that you feel are around you at this time. These types of questions are good to not only learn more about your life in general, but you may discover ways to enhance your life across the board.

4. Be careful how you phrase your questions

Much like avoiding those questions that shift the responsibility, you should also choose vocabulary that will encourage the most amount of guidance. Conditional questions are good for this; for example, "How will my partner feel if I decide to take the promotion?" Your reading will focus more on the emotions of your partner, rather than whether or not you should take the promotion, as that decision is your responsibility.

5. Consider everyone involved

The main goal is to learn more, so that you can make decisions to improve your life, but you still need to consider those who may also be affected by the decision (as with our conditional question). Going back to the promotion, it is likely that the promotion will help get out of the tight money spot. But what if this has negative consequences on your relationship or your other family members?

6. Ask about the advantages and disadvantages

Probably in the past, you have made a list of pros and cons to help you make an important decision. Tarot cards can help you gain better insights into what could be on these two lists. Asking the cards what the advantages and disadvantages of the promotion will provide alternative perspectives.

7. Look for areas of improvement

Maybe you want to expand your skillset, take up a new hobby, or get in shape physically. I know that there is always an area of my life that I would like to work on. Use your readings to ask how you can reach these improvements.

8. Break larger questions down into smaller ones

If you get overwhelmed at the thought of finding a solution to your money worries, it is probable that these emotions will roll over into your reading. Break down the question, so you might want to ask "How can I reduce my spending?" or "What are the advantages of selling this or that?" etc.

9. Keep your questions positive

Even if life isn't going as you had hoped and you are struggling to see the positive in life, you need to keep your readings positive. To help you do this, change any negative questions into a positive. So instead of saying "Why can't I find love?" change the question to "What can I do to find love?".

10. Take notes

There might be things in the reading that you don't understand or that lead you to more questions. It is a great habit to get into making notes of your thoughts and feelings during a reading so that you can reflect on them later. As you are reflecting on your reading, you may discover new questions that you would like further guidance on in the next reading.

You can imagine that it's impossible to list every question you may want to ask in a tarot reading. Each of us has our own concerns, circumstances, and life decisions. We all need to find the questions that will help us on our individual path. Aside from the questions we have seen in the guide above, here are a few more that may give you some inspiration:

- What do I need to be aware of to help me make the right decision?

- What am I missing or ignoring in my life right now?
- What am I doing now that will help me in the future?
- Which steps are the best to take if I want to achieve X,Y,Z?
- What can I learn from my past that will change this situation?
- What do I need to pay more attention to at the moment?
- What is preventing me from achieving my goals?

THE TAROT SPREAD

I can feel the build-up, we are so close to breaking open the deck and giving the cards that all-important shuffle. How do you shuffle tarot cards? Pretty much the same way as a standard deck of cards. I love the way the pros split the pack and fan them together. I tried it and it looked like a game of '78-card pick up'. So, I stick to the over-the-hand shuffle. You can cut the deck into different piles and restack them or just spread them all out on the table and scoop them back into a new pile.

Later on, we will go into more detail about the spread. This is the layout of the cards that are drawn. The simplest layouts are the three-card spread and the five-card spread. Once you get a little more experienced, you can look at the Celtic Cross. You can then have a three-card spread for love, a three-card spread for careers, for understanding the past, etc. When we discuss each card in detail, we will also learn how to read it if it is drawn in the reversed position and its specific meaning.

You may feel that the selection of your cards is a sheer coincidence, but it's far from it. Intuition plays a huge role, even at the point of choosing which cards to draw. This is known as synchronicity or 'meaningful coincidences'. Synchronicity was coined by Jung and he speculated that it was a law of nature that formed part of each person's spiritual development.

It refers to one thing happening at a certain time that has a certain quality or meaning. In Jung's own words, it is the "meaningful connection between the subjective and objective world". He also defined synchronicity as coincidence that appears to exceed random probability.

Examples of what some would say are like a wink from the universe would be dreaming of something specific and then seeing it the following day, seeing repeated numbers, symbols, or colours, even being in the right place at the right time. A few months ago, I was driving when the truck in front of me stopped. Just in front of the truck, there was a horrendous accident. Just minutes earlier, that could have been me, and it wasn't me because I had forgotten my glasses and had to pop back home. I saw this as a sign.

From Jung's point of view, our worldly perceptions and experiences are synchronous with our soul and the images on the cards we draw are intermediaries between ourselves and our spiritual energies. So, even if you consciously try to choose a random card, your current energy will draw you to a particular card and its energy.

WHAT IS THE SIGNIFICATOR?

Though it may sound like something from a sci-fi film, the significator is a card that the reader will choose before a reading. It's certainly not necessary, but for those that are new to tarot, it often helps to draw a deeper connection with the cards, because they can see some meaning in that particular card. This is the card that represents the querent or the thing/person they are asking about. It may even represent the situation you are facing.

In some cases, you might want to choose your significator with intention. With this card next to you during the reading, you will find it easy to relate to the cards. There are a few different ways for you to choose a significator—only if you want to and you feel it will add more value to your reading.

Based on age:

- Children and young adults- A Page
- Young males between 18 and their 30s- A Knight
- Women over 18- A Queen
- Men over 40- A King

Based on astrology:

- Water signs: Cancer, Scorpio, Pisces- Cups
- Fire Signs: Aries, Leo, Sagittarius- Wands
- Air Signs: Gemini, Libra, Aquarius- Swords
- Earth Signs: Taurus, Virgo, Capricorn- Pentacles

Based on appearance:

- Fair skin, blonde hair, blue eyes- Cups
- Rosy complexion, red hair, blue/green eyes- Wands
- Light complexion, light or grey hair, blue/green eyes- Swords
- Dark complexion, dark hair, brown eyes- Pentacles
- Naturally, if you are working on the above descriptions, you can also combine them. In this way, a mature female with blue eyes would choose the Queen of Cups whereas a young man whose star sign is Aries would select the Knight of Wands. If you prefer to choose your significator based on the situation, here is an in-depth guide:
- Love, relationships, family- Cups
- Work, business- Wands
- Disagreements, logic- Swords
- Finance, health- Pentacles
- Fresh starts- The Fool
- Trickery, magic- The Magician
- Psychic ability- The High Priestess
- Parenthood- The Empress
- Advancing your career- The Emperor

- Religion, leaders- The Hierophant
- Love, choices- The Lovers
- Fame, success- The Chariot
- Law, moral, equality- Justice
- Self-discovery, solitude- The Hermit
- Luck- The Wheel of Fortune
- Courage, strength- Strength
- Health- The Hanged Man
- Life-changing decisions- Death
- Peace, calm, happiness- Temperance
- Addictions, obsessions- The Devil
- Unexpected shocks- The Tower
- Hope, desires- The Star
- Doubt, uncertainty- The Moon
- Happiness, family- The Sun
- A calling, destiny- Judgement
- Travel, world issues- The World

Please don't get overwhelmed with another list of meanings. It's a personal preference and you may have done many online searches about tarot and not even heard about the significator until now. My advice would be to try a few readings without one and with one. If you are taking a note of your feelings and thoughts, you will be able to go back over these to see if there is a noticeable difference in your readings.

OOPS, I DROPPED A CARD!

The five-second rule, unfortunately, doesn't apply here, and another thing that I didn't realise until I got deeper into my research is that cards have certain meanings when they are accidentally dropped. I'm also glad I found this out after dropping almost an entire deck, as I was trying to shuffle like they do in the movies. A specific number of dropped cards and whether they land face up (so you can see the image) or face down has important significance.

If you drop…

- One card face up, something related to the card will happen within hours or days.
- One Major Arcana card means you will have a surprise development or something that you haven't been considering will appear in your reading.
- One Court card or Ace points to unexpected news from or related to a relative or authority figure from that suit and you can look forward to a new boost of energy.
- Numbered cards mean a situation (be that good or bad) related to that suit will happen all of a sudden and disappear just as quickly.
- One card face down means the event will occur in the distant future.
- One card face up or down that is drawn in the

reading is the absolute key to everything you need to know.
- Two cards face down suggests there will be two events in the future and one will trigger the next.
- Two cards, one face down and the other face-up means the event of the card facing up will occur beforehand and by paying attention to this, you can minimise any upset from the event of the card facing down.
- Three cards can be used in a three-card spread.

Now, if you have a fumbly-finger day like me and drop more, there is no need to panic. In this case, it's best to pick them up, take a few deep breaths, refocus your mind and start shuffling again. No one is perfect!

MASTERING THE ART OF STORYTELLING

I made it so far without saying 'a picture is worth a thousand words' but it is so true that we have to appreciate this fact. When we master the art of telling the story that appears in the cards, we are going to start seeing some incredible changes in our lives, in the way we feel and how we process our thoughts. We can take these images and use them to make sense of the events in our lives.

Each card represents an archetypal situation that we have experienced throughout our lives. This could be, for example, as the trickster, the saint, or the hero. It may also be in the form of a caregiver, a lover, an artist, or an idealist. We may not remember each of these situations with great clarity, but our experiences are there nevertheless. The art of tarot reading is to appreciate these archetypes through storytelling.

To get better at storytelling, you want to first learn to trust your instincts. You may struggle with this if you have had problems or feel like you have made the wrong decisions in the past. I know what this is like, but try to remember that you aren't the same person and you have learnt from your errors. Your instincts are probably far more in tune now than they were. The more readings you carry out, the more intuitive you will become and the more you will end up discovering. The cards don't hold the secrets, you do.

Enhancing your storytelling skills doesn't have to be limited to when you are using your cards. If you have children, you have the perfect audience. While you are out and about, look at the different situations you see and make up stories with them. Take in the environment and the symbols you may see. Even if you don't have children, you can still take everyday situations and create a story related to it.

As for the cards, don't feel you always have to use them for a reading. Sometimes, you can just select some cards and use the imagery to develop a story. This is a really good exercise for becoming more confident with the symbols and colours. As your confidence and intuition start to grow, you will find it easier to relate these stories to your own life.

In order for you to do this, it's time to take a good look at the amazing imagery of the cards and start to understand more about each specific meaning.

5

THE LANGUAGE OF THE SYMBOLS

In my early, skeptical days, I couldn't see how a psychic was getting so much information from one card. Let's take the Two of Cups as an example. I saw a man and a woman, two cups and a lion head with wings. I paid no attention to the small house in the distance. I never appreciated that the colours brought more meaning, as well as details right down to the displays of wealth on their heads.

Every tiny detail of each tarot card matters and this is why it can take a long time to fully master the art of tarot reading.

THE MEANING OF THE COLOURS

In my book *Modern Chakras*, we paid a lot of attention to the seven chakras and the modern emphasis on the importance of their colour with regards to spiritual healing. You will probably notice some overlaps here and the colours in tarot cards have an insightful power.

White

You may already have made the connection between white and peace, but it is also a sign of innocence and purity. White, and also silver, also represent the light of the moon and femininity. In the Death card, we see white as the colour of cleanings and rebirth, as well as of purity.

White and black

When white is paired with black, it shows absolutes that are present in archetypes. It's the combination of masculine and feminine, or passive and active. The High Priestess sits between a black pillar and a white pillar, showing us that she has found her balance.

White and red

White and red are often seen together in the smaller details, like in flowers or patterns on clothing. These two colours often point to the opposite energies of passion and innocence.

Black

It is less common to find black alone, except in Death and The Devil. It is sometimes seen as bad luck and evil but is more often associated with mystery and the unknown.

Grey

You may find grey pointing to uncertainty or an unhealthy perspective of life. It can be found in cards that have stormy weather and may suggest unhappiness or dullness. In some cases, grey can indicate wisdom.

Red

Red is a passionate and lustful colour. It represents the element of fire, as well as Mercury, Mars, and the suit of Wands. It can also suggest action and inspiration, a passion for life. Sometimes, red will be used for anger and even a strong will. Red is a representation of the conscious mind.

Orange

As a mixture of red (fire) and yellow (air), orange cand be a sign of energetic happiness. It is also a colour that points to enthusiasm, but in some cases, an orange sky could suggest challenges.

Yellow

In the Rider deck, you might see a yellow sky rather than a yellow sun. Sometimes the ground can have a slightly yellow hue rather than brown earth or green grass. It is linked to the masculine energy of the Sun. Yellow is a representation of the highest level of our conscious minds.

. . .

Green

The power of green can tell us of new beginnings, money and well-being. It also has strong ties to the element of Earth, nature, and growth. If you look at all the green in the Queen of Pentacles, you will see the link with living things.

Blue

Generally, blue is a color of inner peace and spirituality. Cards that have a lot of blue are usually related to processes in the subconscious mind. When the figures are wearing blue, it suggests that they are introspective or taking advantage of their subconscious.

Purple

Purple is a very spiritual colour associated with our Third Eye Chakra and psychic energies. You will commonly see it as a colour of wealth, luxury, and royalty.

Pink

On the rare occasions you see pink, it will most probably be in with the Cups. It can be seen as a sign of opulence, sensual pleasure, or unconditional love.

Brown

This is another colour that is associated with earth, but more in the sense of being practical, about working your way through your daily jobs and achieving material success.

Gold

Gold is an amazing healing color and is connected with revitalisation.

Rainbows

If you see a rainbow, it will imply happiness, abundance, and wishes coming true. In other decks, it can be seen as a sign of celebration.

Because there are so many different tarot decks, I won't relate the symbols to any particular card. In the Rider deck, there is no rabbit in the Queen of Pentacles but there is in the Robin Wood deck. Here, we will cover the meanings of the symbols and when we study individual cards, we will look at the symbols combined with colours and meanings.

THE RICH MEANINGS OF THE TAROT SYMBOLS

Angels- messages, divine messages, higher thought and ideas.

- Ankh (Egyptian Cross)- immortality and balance, life, the sun rising from the horizon.
- An arch- entrances, a new direction, taking initiative.
- Armor- protection, being prepared, strength.
- A bench- it's time to sit down, relax, and understand your situation.

- Birds- spiritualism, higher ideas, freedom, ascending to a higher level
- Blindfold- unwilling or unable to see facts and the truth or see things clearly.
- Boats- travel, change in direction, an important thought that will lead us to action.
- Brick wall- negative or inaccurate thinking is holding you back.
- Bridge- Moving from one phase of life to another, we have the resources to help us.
- Bull- power, force, and stability. Also stubbornness and unwillingness to change.
- Butterflies- transformation, often in thoughts, resulting in something beautiful.
- Caduceus (two snakes around a winged staff)- balance, correct moral behavior, protection, cosmic energy, joining forces, new and successful relationships.
- Castle- building strong foundations to reach our goals, shelter, or something preventing us from reaching our goals.
- Cats- perception, a watchful eye, psychic abilities, seeing things from all perspectives.
- Chains- restrictions, conflict, a slave to our own ideas, addition.
- Children- new starts, hope, promises, a sign of the future, a new venture or literally, the birth of a child.
- City or village- centers and people, thoughts, and energies coming together in a group effort.

Protection, the need for teamwork and tapping into the energy of others.
- Clouds- confusion, clouded judgement, higher thoughts, divine messages, or the contrary, a revelation or epiphany.
- Dogs- loyalty, honesty, righteousness, often a sign that we are on the right path or that we need to question our loyalties.
- Doves- purity, hope, ascending, love. When the dove is pointing down, it reminds us to be grounded before we take to the sky.
- Falcon- higher vision, vibrancy, power, we may question whether or not we are reaching our potential.
- Fire- energy, passion, ambition, and power. It has the power to destroy and create.
- Fish-emotions, intuition, unpredictable motion in our subconscious, abundance is you can control our passions.
- Flag- the announcement of a change, but the change will depend on the imagery on the flag.
- Flowers- unfolding and opening up, receiving joy and love, the beauty that is all around is.
- Globes- the union of the cosmic and the physical, achievement is nearby, seeing the bigger picture, completion and cycles.
- Grapes or grapevines- this fruit has powerful meanings for different religions: fertility, redemption, hospitality or youthfulness.

- Hammer- hammer your point, hammer the detail, force, action and masculinity.
- Hand- giving and receiving from one hand to the next, power, domination and protection.
- Heart- aside from love and affection, truth, the center of our being and existence.
- Hoe- hard work and effort, resourcefulness, we reap what we sow— the good and the bad.
- Horn- a triumphant or victorious announcement, or possibly a warning.
- Horses- strength, action, vitality, a symbol of spirituality and incorporation of the elements.
- A house- our own sacred place, where we hold our closest secrets, safety and protection.
- Ice- isolation, distance, patience, profound contemplation, growth that won't be seen till later.
- Keys- unlocking our knowledge, intellect, wisdom, potential, or is our potential being locked away.
- Lantern- illumination, truth, a symbol of life, vigilance, clarity.
- Lemniscate (infinity symbol)- infinite energy that can't be created or destroyed, thoughts and actions where the consequence could be infinite.
- Lightning- instant divine intervention, a creative spark, the creator and the destroyer.
- Lily- purity, fertility, health, growth, vulnerability, confidence to be ourselves.

- Lion- strength, courage, royalty, protection, spiritual valor, our saviour or our destroyer.
- Lizard or salamander- renewal, rebirth, enlightenment, vision, small conscious efforts lead to big changes.
- Lobster, crab or crayfish- lunar symbols, cycles, rebirth, casting shells, protection.
- Moon- femininity, levels of awareness, intuition, reflection, phases, a powerful influence.
- Mountains- obstacles, success, attainment, realization, endurance, everlasting, consider our place in the universe.
- Ocean- vastness, depth, infinite possibilities, the power that surrounds us, a reminder that we aren't always in control, possibilities.
- Path- direction, phases of life, beginnings and endings, small steps make progress.
- Pillars- balance, diplomacy, strategy, things aren't black or white, the middle way can provide new perspectives.
- Pitcher- a vessel, the contents of our mind or heart, the need to be a pure vessel.
- Plowed fields- We reap what we sow, the efforts we make impact our harvest, patience, time.
- Pomegranates- plentiful, fertility, love, female sexuality, feminine power, luxuries and wonders in the world.
- Rabbit- grounding, social, good judgement, fast-acting.

- Rain- cleansing, wash away the old to make way for the new, providing life.
- Ram- taking initiative, action, determination, motivation, leadership, taking responsibility.
- Ropes- restriction, binding, being in a knot, state of inaction, struggling makes the knots tighter.
- Rose- beauty, purity, new beginnings, hope, thorn pricks represent potential pain.
- Scale- equality, balance, where we need to create more balance in our lives.
- Scroll- passing down of sacred knowledge, secrets, hidden facts.
- Shield- protection from what can harm us and what we value.
- Ship- journeys, water, the subconscious, emotional baggage on your voyage.
- Snail- slow and steady progress, security and happiness being carried with us.
- Snake- renewal, the need to adapt and be flexible, shed things so we can grow.
- Snow- quiet, beauty, fresh, crystally, beauty, a choice between being left in the cold or enjoying the beauty.
- Sphinx- guardianship, protecting life's secrets, using our senses, unraveling secrets.
- Staff- support by the archetypes, stability, represents the number 1, new beginnings.
- Stained glass- perception and beliefs impact our vision, clear vision or rose-coloured glasses.

- Star- illumination, guidance, direction from a higher source.
- Sun- energy, growth, expansion, the rising sun represents new beginnings, midday for creativity, setting for an ending or a transformation.
- Sunflower- looking to the bright side, positivity.
- Tomb- lay to rest the things that are no longer any use, changing mindsets.
- Triangle- balance, creativity, intelligence, the energy of love, the union of the mother, father, child.
- Wall- keeping parts of our lives separate, privacy.
- Waterfall- constant flow of emotions, emotions crashing to the ground or running away from us, the need to control our emotions.
- Wolf- primal urges, loyalty, intelligence, refocus desires, being true to ourselves.
- Wreath- victory, protection, peace, purification.

It's an incredible list when you think about it. One part of the cards is about appreciating these symbols, but the other part is then deciphering which of the possible meanings each symbol will have. This could be helped by combinations of different symbols on a tarot card or the cards that come before or after.

MINOR ARCANAS AND THE SIGNIFICANCE OF NUMBERS

Some people have lucky numbers. For example, some won't change their lottery numbers, because they are "the lucky numbers"—despite never winning! Others count magpies, because the number they see is a sign (remember '1 for sorrow, 2 for joy'). I know people who won't stay in certain hotel rooms because of the number, even hotel owners who skip room numbers. Whether you believe in numerology or not, numbers have and will continue to play an important role in our belief systems. Here is what the numbered cards mean in a tarot deck:

The Ones- The aces are represented by the number one and are a sign of pure energy. This energy needs to be shaped and you have to take great care to do so that you gain the most from it. Without care, the power of this energy can overwhelm you.

The Twos- The solitude of the ace is left behind as we move onto unions between two people. More often than not, twos represent a peaceful joining of two people, even when the forces are opposite. There are occasions when the connection between two people is so strong that it is hard to break free from it when certain decisions have to be made.

The Threes- Like in many religions and cultures, three signifies a group, whether that's people, objects, or ideas.

We frequently associate three with grouping in order to complete a phase, but lookout for creative moments.

The Fours- Before you can build a house, you need the four corners of the foundation. The same can be said for many things, that the fountain is crucial for growth. The fours are telling us that endurance is necessary for us to progress, despite the disappointments we may have.

The Fives- The theme of pushing forward continues from the threes. The fives often tell us that change or turbulence is present. There is a need to take our energy and use it to overcome conflicts and the reasons that cause us to doubt change. The answers are more often than not found within you.

The Sixes- Our disagreements with ourselves or with others are about to convert into solutions. If you draw a six, you may have to resolve issues you have with people or learn how to let go of things that no longer benefit you. A six is a sign of positivity after times of difficulty.

The Sevens- One of the sevens in a reading suggests your best course of action might be some time to yourself to reflect on what it is really is that you want to achieve. Take some time for introspection so that you consider if you are on the path you should be on.

The Eights- You can expect a second phase to come to completion, because you are mastering your skills. There may even be an achievement that will help to further your growth. Your success might be a physical one or an emotional one, and you may find that it comes about when you least expect it.

The Nines- Though close to the end and these cards may suggest the end of your cycle is near, they could also be a sign that this is a pause before the final change or achievement. Life's events may level off before you reach your goal. There may be more to come.

The Tens- Drawing a ten is another sign of moving forward, but in these cases, it is because your cycle has reached competition. The full circle has come around and now it is time to look forward to those new beginnings.

It's true that the Major Arcanas also have their individual numerical numbers, but rather than create another section here, I think it is better to cover this when we look at each card individually and in more depth.

A SUIT FOR EACH ELEMENT

I have already touched on the different elements for each suit, but because it has been embedded with other information, I'd like to save a mini section to help reinforce what we have already seen, plus to outline the link between each one and the seasons.

The Cups are related to the element water, and this ties in with our emotions and intuition. The cups often point to our relationships and creativity. There is often a great amount of joy with the Cups as they represent summer, the warmth of those longer days and feeling complete.

As the earth element is seen in the Pentacles, we can appreciate a link to material wealth, healthy finances and careers. Things start to manifest when the Pentacles are drawn. There is a logical connection between the Pentacles and autumn/fall as this is the season when we can harvest our plentiful crops.

Air is the known element for the Swords and this suit is a sign of thoughts and intellect. Furthermore, it is a sign of truth and communication. There is a lot of sadness in the images of these cards, some are cold and lonely, and so the Swords represent winter.

As the cycle of the seasons comes back around, the Wands, represented by the element of fire, are symbols of spring. Spring is a time for enthusiasm, energy, and new beginnings. Notice how new life blossoms from the Wands.

TAROT SYMBOLOGY AND WITCHCRAFT

Black cats, tall hats, and bats are strung up as decorations for Halloween, but are far from the symbols that most practising witches associate with. There are plenty of examples of relationships between symbols of the tarot cards and symbols in witchcraft.

The most obvious is the pentacle or pentagram. The five-pointed star inside a circle represents the four elements (the four lower points) and the final point of the star represents the spirit. The star, sun, and moon are all present in both practices. But then, if you start to look a little closer, you will notice the link with symbols like snakes, flowers and wreaths. In many ways, the tarot cards and witchcraft complement each other.

It's been a bit of a listicle chapter, but this was necessary to get a true understanding of the depth of imagery within the cards. If, like me, you would look at a card and only see the surface, I hope that with the help of these lists, you will be able to draw more meaning from the different symbols, colours, and numbers. Now that you are aware of the powerful imagery, we can begin working on the different types of tarot spreads.

6

OPTIMISE YOUR SPREADS

There are numerous tarot card spreads that you can use in a reading. The main reason for such a variety is that each situation will require a different type of spread. You can't imagine a love spread providing the same insight as a sibling-rivalry spread. Even when looking at love spreads, you will be able to see a relationship cross spread, which is one of the more straightforward ones, to a ready for love spread, requiring more cards. Some spreads are designed to give you faster guidance, like the Yes/No spread, but you can also do a more detailed reading with a twelve-month spread.

Many times, one type of spread can be used with different intentions. The three-card spread can be used to uncover general insights, in which case we call it a non-dedicated spread. A dedicated spread would still have three cards, but it would be about love, your career, or something else more specific.

Like with everything else we have talked about regarding tarot cards, it is a case of practising the different types of spreads and finding which ones you find yourself connecting too more. It is better to stick to the easier spreads while you are gaining more confidence with the symbolism and then move onto spreads that require more cards.

Because the layout of the cards is so crucial, I have included some diagrams at the end of the book that you can copy or print and keep close by while you are learning. For now, I am going to rely on my creative explanations to guide you through some of the most important spreads you can try.

Before you start randomly picking cards, let's just remind ourselves of the basics. I hate being repetitive, but the preparation is essential for the right results. Things like lighting a candle, meditative music, etc., are up to you, I'm talking about the fundamentals:

- Make sure you are in a calm environment where you can focus and won't be interrupted
- Calm your mind, let go of the negative thoughts and start to bring your mind towards the question you want to ask
- Shuffle your cards (you don't have to be a pro, nobody is examining you). It is essential that you

shuffle the cards before every read. This is to cleanse the cards of the previous questions

And for the new stuff... hold the cards in both hands and focus on your question. Cut the cards with your left hand and place the bottom pile on the top. From this point, you have the first card for your tarot card spread. I try not to be biased in my books and generally exclude my favourites, but in this case, I will start with two of my preferred spreads for when I was first learning. After that, I have added the most popular tarot spreads and tried to keep them in order of simplicity.

One Card Tarot Spread

It doesn't get much easier than this, but it isn't really designed to provide detailed guidance. We would use a one-card tarot spread more often in daily use. It's like a short meditation session about your day. I prefer to use this in the morning so that I can make better decisions throughout the day. Take the first card in your prepared deck and see what the images are telling you.

Three Card Tarot Spread

This is probably one of the most common spreads for beginners and for tarot readers because it can be less overwhelming. However, the forms can vary, so again, you need to have your question clear. A three-card spread might be about the past, present and future. Other spreads could focus on the foundation, problem, and advice. The Yes/No/Maybe is also a popular form. Take the first three cards and lay them from left to right. The first card may represent your concern, the second the obstacle and the resolution (as an example).

Simple Five Tarot Card Spread

It's another great option and I found there was a nice easy transition from the three-card spread to the five-card spread. By adding two more cards, you naturally get a better understanding of your question. The first card is the general meaning of the spread, the second looks to past events, and the third points to the future. The fourth one will tell you more about the reason behind the question. It's normal to find some relation between the second and forth card, like 'the penny dropped' moment. The fifth card looks at the potential within the situation.

Seven Day Tarot Card Spread

I like this one because it is like an extended version of the one day spread. You would lay seven cards from left to right and an eighth card above card number seven. Each of the seven cards represents a day, with the first corresponding with the day of your reading. The eighth card is an overview of the week. Don't forget the intention of your question. Do you want a general look at the week ahead or are you looking for specific guidance to your job?

Seven Card Horseshoe Spread

Those with experience drop their jaws as I talk about this spread before others that are more common, but I have always felt that this is still incredibly insightful, but just a tad less daunting. The seven-card horseshoe spread starts with the first card positioned at the top left of the spread and the following cards are positioned in a horseshoe shape or 'V' with the fourth card being the tip of the 'V'. The first card looks to the past and the second at the present. The third card points to hidden influences and don't worry if you find it hard to see the significance straight away. The fourth card is a representation of you whereas the fifth focuses on the influence of those around you. The sixth card indicates what you should do and the final, seventh card implies the outcome.

Six Month Tarot Card Spread

It's very similar to the seven day spread, but for a longer period of time. As the layout is the same, it is essential that your focus and intention are for the full six months. Cards one to six are placed from left to right and the first card shows the month you are currently in. Each card can give you insights into the months ahead. The seventh card, placed in the top right corner will help you to see the full six months more clearly.

The Romany tarot Card Spread

This spread requires twenty-one cards in three rows, seven cards in each. Despite having a lot of cards, this is still quite a simple spread which will tell you more about the various stages in your life. The first seven cards in the top row offer insight into your past. The second row of seven indicates what is happening in the present. And the bottom row points to the future if the middle row continues as it is. You can use this for both general and specific readings.

CHAKRA BALANCE TAROT CARD SPREAD

It goes without saying that I have also loved this one, because of how much I gained from learning about my chakras and keeping them balanced. So, this spread is another great tool to work in conjunction with the chakras. Cards one to seven are placed in a vertical row. The first represents the Root Chakra, the second, the Root Chakra, and so on. Each card will provide insights into whether the chakra is overactive, underactive, or balanced.

The Celtic Cross Tarot Spread

While it comes out on top for popularity, the number of cards and placements may put some beginners off. The first card, placed in the center, shows your influences at the time. The second is placed horizontally on top of the first and indicates what is blocking you. You need to place the third card below the first; this is the past which has created the foundations for where you are today. The fourth card sits to the left of the first and deals with your past from further back. Above the first card you would place card number five, a representation of your dreams, and to the right of the first card is the sixth, and this card hints to your future. To the right of the spread, you need to lay cards seven to ten (bottom to top) in a vertical row.

These cards are signs of your attitude towards the situation, how others see you, your hopes or fears, and the outcome, respectively.

Snapshot Tarot Card Spread

This is a good one, because the snapshot gives you a look at your emotions, as well as aspects from your spiritual and mental life in the past, present and future, plus the opportunity to see how they are linked. Lay cards one to three from left to right on the table. This shows your emotional, mental, and spiritual pasts. The fourth card is placed above the second and looks at the power of your past. Cards five, six, and seven (from left to right) are placed above the fourth card (card six directly above). Like the first three, they look at the emotional, mental and spiritual aspects but in the present. The eighth card shows the power of the present and is placed above the sixth. The final row on top of the eighth card (nine, ten, eleven) are the emotional, mental, and spiritual aspects of your life in the future. The last card, number twelve, is placed above the tenth and is the snapshot of the life cycle you are in at present.

I always feel that when I get to the end of a chapter, I reinforce my own realisation that the cards are hard to learn. I feel blessed that I stuck at it and took the time to learn not just the imagery but also the benefits of the different spreads. That being said, I do remember a time at the beginning where I just stuck in the habit of only doing three and five card spreads. Even when my confidence increased, I still feared the idea of trying a new spread. Don't make the same mistake as I did. While it's good to practice with the easier spreads, not trying out the more intricate ones could mean that you miss out on some amazing guidance.

There is still a deeper connection between witchcraft and tarot cards, including a particular spread that I would like to explore a little more with you. If you are in touch with the witch (or wizard) inside of you, you will enjoy the last chapter in part one. If you are still a little skeptical of witchcraft, that's ok too. I only hope that you keep reading with an open mind as we uncover the incredible relationships we have with the elements and other concepts we see in the cards.

7

A LITTLE BIT OF WITCHCRAFT TO GET YOU STARTED

Picture this, you learnt Spanish at school and have tried to keep up with at least the basics. Your boss offers you the chance to move to Italy and it dawns on you that you are going to have to learn a new language. Now imagine your relief when you notice there are some similarities between the languages. The same thing happens with tarot and witchcraft: once you start mastering one, you can see the beautiful links with the other.

There is no need to rehash the links between the witchcraft, tarot and the four elements air, fire, earth and water. By now, you may have also picked on the overlap between three of the suits, the wands, cups, and pentacles. We saw the power of numbers that the cards represent and numerology is also a practice closely tied to the occult, as is astrology. There are three main reasons why you might want to consider using tarot cards along with your witchcraft practices:

1. By performing a tarot reading before you cast a spell, you will be better informed about what lays ahead for you.
2. Certain cards can be used in a spell to incorporate more energy into it. If you are planning a spell related to prosperity you might want to include the King of Pentacles or a spell to overcome the challenges you face would be helped with the Chariot card.
3. Using tarot cards when casting spells will help with your visualisation, particularly if you can relate figures in the cards to certain people.

Casting spells can be used for good and for bad. I am not here to judge or tell you what to do, but I do not use the power of the cards or spells to do harm. First of all, I have no intention of wasting my time on people who have hurt me and secondly, I don't want that negative energy around me. If tempted to put a curse on someone for their actions, try to understand where their actions are coming from. It's more than likely that they have some underlying issues in their life and this is causing them to react in the wrong way. You could choose to be the better person and try to find or create a spell that will help them. But again, it's up to you!

I have one more list for you regarding the cards you can use to help you create your spells. The following will give you a better idea of which cards are more suited to certain spells. Remember it is just a general list and I encourage you to find your own personal connections with the cards for spell casting, once you are more familiar with them.

- To create action- The Chariot, Ace/Eight of Wands
- To change a bad habit- Strength, Temperance, Judgement
- To find inspiration or creativity- The Magician, The Star, The Moon
- For success in a project-The Magician, The Sun, Ace of Wands
- For business success- The Sun, Three of Wands, Ace of Pentacles
- For a change- The Magician, Wheel of Fortune, Eight of Wands
- For fertility- The Empress, The Sun, Ten of Cups
- For help making a decision- The Hermit, The Star, Justice
- To break free from guilt and suffering- Judgement, The World, The Moon
- To bind your spells- The Hanged Man, Temperance, Two of Swords
- To promote healing and good health- The Sun, Strength, The Star, Three of Cups
- To enhance wisdom and knowledge- The Hermit, High Priestess, The Moon

- To bring about financial wealth- Ace/Six/Ten/Courts of Pentacles
- When you need protection- Temperance, The Chariot, Four of Wands
- For self-improvement- The Magician, Strength, The World
- To relieve stress and anxiety- Temperance, Ace/Four of Cups

HOW EXACTLY DO YOU CREATE A SPELL?

If you have read my other books, you probably know how much I love my analogies and cooking. So, creating a spell is just like creating your own recipe. You might find a recipe for lasagne and it turns out OK, and this could happen when you use a prewritten spell. But when you tweak the ingredients to match your own tastes, your result is going to excel—all you need is the basic outline. In this section, we are going to look at the basic outline for creating your own spell.

Your purpose and words

We have covered purpose and intention, but here we will put these into words to make sure you achieve the right outcomes. Spells rarely go wrong, but they don't always turn out as we had hoped, because we haven't taken the time to choose the correct vocabulary. A perfect example is when you cast a spell for more money and the next day your boss asks you to do overtime—you got more money, but probably not how you were thinking!

Avoid words like will and want, pain, fear, no, and contractions (can't, don't, etc.) Imagine how you would feel and what you would be doing if you were in the situation you wish to use the spell for. Your spell and your heart might say "I don't want to be fat", but a more specific and positive spell would be "I am strong and I am healthy".

Note the use of the present tense. When we cast our spell into the universe, it isn't able to decipher between the past, present, and the future. For the universe, all we have is now. The present tense tells both your subconscious and the universe that you are ready for this change now. For more inspiration, you can see the section called Affirmations in Healing Mantras.

This is not a Disney film, or any other spell to entertain the viewers, so don't feel that it has to rhythm or sound good to a tune. Spells are best not shared in case the energy of the person in some way impacts the spell.

Once you are happy with your words, say the spell out loud and get a sense of how it sounds to you. If you like it, write it down. Bit by bit, you can create your own personal book of spells, some you will be able to adjust for different moments in the future.

The materials you can use

I can't stress this part enough: materials will help, especially if you are a little skeptical or if you feel like you need some extra help from components that you can use in a spell, but they are not necessary. It hurt me to see one young gentleman spend practically all of his income on materials for his spells and he ended up in more problems than before. Build up a spell kit slowly—a herb here and a candle there. And if you can't afford it, all you need is your mind. In fact, psychic spells never require objects or even words, just focus! Here are some things that you may want to gradually add to your kit:

Stones and crystals- Each crystal has its own energy and power (red jasper for strength, black tourmaline for protection, amazonite for confidence). You can use them in protection circles and at the altar and later carry them around with you. Look for crystals that are attractive to you. Each type of crystal will come in different shapes, textures and tones. Also, you need to cleanse your crystal before you use it and recharge it. You can do both of these things by running your crystal under water or submerging it in fresh saltwater and then leaving it in the sunlight and moonlight to recharge—only if it isn't sensitive to water or light.

Herbs- I killed two birds with one stone and grew a little herb garden for spells and cooking, but many people find it more convenient to use dried herbs. Spearmint is ideal in spells for courage, garlic wards off negativity, and witch hazel can help mend a broken heart.

Essential Oils- Both oils and incense work in a similar way to herbs. As we breathe in the scents, our brain receives certain messages. Aromatherapy has been used in healing for centuries for the positive effects it can purportedly trigger.

Candles- The best thing about candles is that we all probably have one or two in our homes anyway. It is also very easy to buy such a huge range of candles, so you can choose curtain ones that really compliment your spell. A red, rose-scented candle is perfect for a love spell. You can also combine candles with essential oils to create your own scented candle. If you are calling upon the element of fire, a candle may help.

Other tools- I say the word cauldron and it immediately causes people to laugh and, because of commercialism, some people feel that it is a bit gimmicky, but it is the perfect tool for mixing herbs. You may choose to use a chalice instead. Again, a Tupperware pot will also work, so don't feel compelled to buy these tools if you can't or don't want to.

THE TIMING OF YOUR SPELL

Not every situation will allow us to wait for the perfect moment to cast a spell. This is more of a little bonus idea that can give your spell a boost of power. Also, not every spell will correlate to an ideal time. Each day of the week corresponds to a celestial body in the solar system and each planet has its own energetic properties:

- Monday- the Moon- psychic abilities, dreams, feminine energy, fertility, family

- Tuesday- Mars- energy, motion, independence, overcoming obstacles, handling conflicts
- Wednesday- Mercury- knowledge, creativity, communication, education, careers
- Thursday- Jupiter- business, finances, prosperity, legal issues
- Friday- Venus- love, relationships, sexuality, marriage, social status
- Saturday- Saturn- meditation, binding, overcoming habits, discipline, protection
- Sunday- The Sun- health, happiness, strength, general success

Finally, certain spells will benefit from the phase the Moon is in.

- New Moon- fresh beginnings, health and beauty, personal and/or professional growth
- Waxing Moon- motivation and inspiration, friendships, healing, personal strength, luck
- Full Moon- creativity, romance, love, fertility, psychic abilities and divination
- Waning Moon- overcoming bad habits or addictions, ending unhealthy relationships

BRINGING YOUR SPELL TOGETHER

Not wanting to moan about the negative impact of the film and TV industry again, but casting a spell isn't just about lighting a candle and chanting a rhyme. From start to finish, from my intention to researching the particular materials, I am rarely able to create a new spell in less than twenty to thirty minutes. Sometimes, it can take hours to get it right. Maybe those who practise spells and consult their own book can do it faster, but everybody would agree, you can't rush his process. Here is how I created a tarot wish spell:

I was having some difficulty with a friend and we couldn't see eye-to-eye on a moral matter. I wanted to bring some more harmony and joy back into our friendship. First, I collected:

- The Three of Cups card
- A white candle
- A clear quartz crystal
- A piece of white string

I felt that the following words summed up how I wanted our friendship to be:

"We are kind, intelligent, loving people and we understand each other's points of view".

Next, I tied the string around the card and placed it next to the candle that I then lit. I held the crystal in my hand and imagined myself and my friend in a happy celebration. Once I could clearly see us in this place, I said my spell. Then I left my crystal on top of the card until the candle burnt down. For the tarot Wish Spell, you need to put the card under your pillow while you sleep until your wish comes true.

A TAROT SPREAD FOR WITCHCRAFT

Another perfect union of tarot cards and witchcraft is the Pentagram spread. This spread looks at the four elements, plus a fifth—the spirit—which completes the five points of the pentagram.

Place the first card in the center. This card is the significator. The next five cards will be placed on each point of the star around the significator, say one o'clock, five o'clock, seven o'clock, ten o'clock and twelve o'clock. The card at one o'clock is the earth element and looks at our security. It will represent the problem you face. At five 0'clock, you have the element of air and relates to communication. It can provide insight into what others are telling you or how they are influencing you. The card at seven o'clock is connected to fire, and don't forget its ability to both create and destroy. This card may point to the doubts you have, an internal conflict, or even ways that you are destroying your own goals. Next, at ten 0'clock, we have water, the element of wisdom. There are things you can learn from this situation, more so when you listen to your intuition. Finally, at the highest point of the pentagram, we have the spirit element. This card will show you the end result of all your influences and ultimately the result if you remain on the path you are on.

USING TAROT CARDS TO HELP WITH CIRCLE CASTING

Circle casting or a magic circle is a little bit like a safety bubble. It's a psychic boundary that is cast for protection, but also serves for other purposes. Your magic circle will protect you by filtering the negative energies and only allowing the positive energy to pass through. It can also help by protecting you from distractions. This protective barrier will also help to contain your energy and even amplify it.

It is not necessary to cast a circle before a spell, but it is a ritual that many people follow, especially in the early days when we are developing our focus and intuition. If you do decide to cast a magic circle, here are the steps to follow:

1. Find a flat space that allows for a circle of about five to six feet in diameter. Indoors or outdoors is fine but it has to be somewhere quiet.
2. Identify the four cardinal points. Remember the sun rises in the east and sets in the west, or cheat and use the compass on your phone.
3. Take one tarot card that represents each of the four elements and place them on the corresponding cardinal point.
4. In each of the following, take a deep breath, relax, and feel a connection with the words:

- Face east and say, "Spirits of Air, I call on you"

- Turn south and say, "Spirits of Fire, I call on you"
- Turn west and say, "Spirits of Water, I call on you"
- Finally, face north and say, "mother Earth, I call on you", then draw the energy of the cosmos into your body and say, "Father Sky, I call on you".
- Finish by showing your gratitude and say, "Thank you, the circle is cast, blessed be".

1. Your sacred area is now ready for you to focus on your magic.
2. Once you have finished, be sure to repeat step four but instead, thank each of the elements, for example, "Air, you were here, and I thank you for this". When you have completed your circle of gratitude, the magic circle will release the energy that has been contained within it.

Congratulations on this mammoth amount of information you have taken on. As soon as I started to see the power of the images and symbols combined with the complexities of different spreads, I began to understand why seasoned professionals charged what they did for a tarot reading. Though it might feel like you are back at school and you will never remember it all, trust me, you will and it won't be long until you start to feel your intuition growing and you feel more confident in the decisions you make that will keep you on the right path to achieve your goals. Don't forget to have fun while you are doing this and to make it enjoyable, explore different methods and tools. The possibilities are infinite!

PART II

In the following part of *Modern Tarot*, we are going to break down each card and look at their general meanings. It will then be up to you to combine the general meaning with the information in Part 1, so for example, your particular question and spread.

When it comes to adding crystals, oils, herbs and candles, I am going to encourage you to do your own research. This isn't because I am lazy or I don't know. But from experience, when someone tells me this or that works, I go out and buy it, because my brain thinks I must need it. I don't want you to hear seventy-eight different crystals, oils, herbs and candles and feel an obligation to buy them. There are also many tools that can be used for more than one intention and so with your own experience and research, you will be able to create a personalised kit.

Don't forget that I am using my trusted Rider-Waite deck to describe the figures and images in each card. With that in mind, let's begin!

THE MAJOR ARCANA TAROT CARDS

The twenty-two Major Arcana cards are representations of our bigger life events or decisions. They represent a story of personal development and growth. The beginning of our journey starts with the innocence of youth.

The Fool

Don't assume the young man in the card is an idiot. The term 'fool' refers to his innocence or lack of judgement, emphasised by the puppy at his feet. Notice the white rose in his hand, another symbol of innocence and purity. He is not scared of anything on the edge of the cliff and the bright yellow sky radiates positivity. The bag over his shoulder suggests he is about to go on a journey, which could relate to your situation.

Reversed- Innocence comes with its problems. One more step and the Fool could be in danger. You should fear the next stage you are about to take on, but you should pay close attention to everything that is around you.

The Magician

The colours red and white are very predominant, along with the yellow background. The red and white show the purity of his magic. The Magician represents balance, with one hand pointing to the sky and the other to the earth, and completion, seen in the infinity symbol over his head. There is a cup, wand, sword, and pentacle on the table to his right—the righteous side. He is confident that he can bring these four symbols together as he looks ahead to the future. Like the Magician, you may have learnt new skills.

Reversed- The new skills you have learnt might be of the manipulative kind or perhaps you like to show others skills that you haven't mastered yet. If you know someone in your life who likes to control you, now might be the time to keep some distance.

The High Priestess

The High Priestess sits on a throne between a black and a white pillar, a sign of the beginning and the end. The High Priestess is a wise woman, seen by the large pearl on her crown. But this wisdom isn't necessarily what the world has taught her. Her robes are blue, the colour of intuition. This card points to our inner wisdom. Behind the throne, there is ripe fruit, a symbol of fertility and even prosperity. If you want to reach this place, know that your journey will have to take you through the pillars.

Reversed- In this position, you may find you aren't listening to your intuition or other people's opinions are having too much sway over you. Maybe someone has too much power over your thoughts and feelings, stopping your creativity.

The Empress

Just look at all of the symbols in this card! There is a stream, a field full of life, the symbol of Venus. The pomegranates on her robe are ready to harvest and her crown is made of stars, her link to the higher world. The Empress is comfortable with her beauty, her sexuality, and her creativity. While this card is often a sign of fertility, it also reminds us of the beauty in the world. It can also indicate the growth of material goods.

Reversed- We often assume that the reversal means a lack of fertility, but it is more likely that you are struggling to appreciate your femininity. If you draw this card upturned, you may need to start putting your needs before those of others.

The Emperor

The curved, comforting thrones of the High Priestess and the Empress have been replaced with a stone throne with straight, solid edges, much more masculine. The sky is a darker red, more like fire. The scepter in his right-hand looks like an ankh. The Emperor is obviously wiser than the Fool. There is a combination of intuition (just a hint of blue clothing) and protectiveness (his armour covering his feet and legs). This card means that you have probably gained and even though this might not be much, it still needs to be protected. You have what it takes to achieve your goals.

Reversed- Never abuse the power you have gained or be careful of acting as if you have more control over things than you actually do. Make sure you are setting the right example and not expecting others to do things you aren't willing to do.

The Hierophant

The Hierophant is the leader of the religious world, represented by the three tiers of his crown and the closeness to heaven. Two monks face him, one wearing a robe of red flowers, the other white. The Hierophant wears a combination of red and white. He seems to be educating the monks, perhaps performing a ceremony. Your education is important when this card appears. You may have a strong mentor in your life who will guide you on your journey.

Reversed- Depending on your situation, you might feel the need to rebel against the tradition that we often see in long-standing institutions. If your mentor doesn't have your best interests at heart, you may need to look in other directions for guidance.

The Lovers

It's hard not to see the correlation with Adam and Eve before the fall: they are naked, but show no shame, the trees are full of fruit and the snake is wrapped around the tree behind the woman. Some will see the river as a sign of the lovers coming together, others see the mountain between them as the challenges that keep them apart. The Sun offers warmth and the angel who towers over them has large red wings and purple robes. More often than not, this card points to romantic relationships, but it can also point to the other relationships in your life that are equal.

Reversed- Your relationship might be lacking balance, one of you may be feeling a lack of appreciation. Equality isn't limited to tasks in the house, it also extends to your love and caring for each other.

The Chariot

The man in the chariot looks as if he has accomplished things on his travels and you could see this as a sign that you will too. He is strong and determined, as well as in touch with his spiritual side. He has made his way alone and if you are determined, so can you. Will power drivers the chariot. On the front of the chariot, there are blue wings and in front, a black and a white sphinx. Look very closely at his shoulders. His armored suit appears to have two moons, one happy and the other sad.

Reversed- If you aren't moving at full speed, you might need an extra dose of courage, focus, or determination. Don't depend on others or material objects. The tie spent in looking for other people's approval could be better spent alone.

Strength

I love the combination of the beauty of the female figure with the masculinity of the lion. This combination is the key—we can all have a wild side and a feminine side. Despite being the king of the jungle, the lion still has his tail between his legs. Once again, we see three key colours, the woman is wearing white, the lion is red, and the sky is a bright yellow. Strength in this card doesn't come from tools or weapons but in will and kindness. You may be tempted to run from your challenges, but if you can be calm, you can succeed.

Reversed- Most problems we can overcome, but upturned, your troubles may be getting the better of you, because you don't feel like you have the power or ability to overcome them. Take care that the lions in your life aren't draining your strength.

The Hermit

There is a noticeable difference in the colours used in this card. The white hair suggests he has become wiser, while the white snow reminds of our innocence. His gray robes suggest he can now see things in more than just black and white. The Hermit is very much alone and although the scene looks quite dull, he is taking the time to self-reflect. The wand in his left hand suggests he knows things that others don't. This card often means you need to take a step back from the hustle and bustle so that you can find some peace.

Reversed- On the contrary, in the reserved position may imply that you are too focused on yourself. You may have alienated people, because you feel you are above them, but the Hermit chooses to be alone.

Wheel of Fortune

Where do we begin? You can see the four elements in the middle of the wheel, letters around the rim, four figures in the corners, each having a relationship with a zodiac sign. Hermes, a snake, and a sphinx are all balanced on the wheel. As the wheel turns, evil will fall as wisdom rises, but because life is one big cycle, as the wheel turns, evil will rise again. You will have ups and downs, but your luck will change, so it's important to stay positive.

Reversed- If you feel like you are down on your luck, you need to take responsibility for your actions to make a change. Some people get stuck in the past and aren't able to change. Be careful of negative attitudes and self-fulling prophecies.

Justice

Justice wears a rich red robe and a golden cloak. Her crown has just one blue gem in the middle and this is in line with the blue gem in her cloak—a more subtle sign of balance. In her left hand, she has the signature balanced scales, in her right, a double-edged sword. She is the definition of fairness, but the white shoe just appearing from under her robe is a reminder that we are innocent until proven guilty. If you feel like you have been treated unfairly, this might be rectified soon. Those who lie and cheat will get what is coming to them.

Reversed- I assumed that it would mean injustice, but no, it actually still implies justice, but that this isn't always clear and there may be a price to pay. Justice is the right thing, but it may come at a cost or a sacrifice.

The Hanged Man

The name always brought a bit of a chill down my spine, but don't assume the worst. First of all, the young man is hanging from one foot. He has gold shoes, red trousers and a blue shirt. A halo glows around his head. The sky is quite bleak, but there are green leaves growing off the cross he is tied to. The card can have different meanings for different readers. Some will assume that his hands are tied behind his back and it's a helpless situation. Others feel that he doesn't look distressed. The halo suggests he is spiritually aware, but he could be difficult to trust with his hands behind his back. His bent leg looks like the number four, a symbol of the four elements.

Reversed- You need to free yourself from what is restricting you. Perhaps you feel like you don't have what it takes to untie yourself. If you don't take action or make a decision, some else may do it for you.

Death

It's normal to think the worst—both the name and the imagery can be shocking. Drawing the Death card isn't a sign that someone is about to die! Instead, it points to the end of something or that you are heading for a big change. Death is riding a white horse and the black banner has a white rose, signs of purity. Although the people seem to be working through the stages of grief, there is still plenty of life in the imagery. There is a river, trees, and the Sun still rises, so life goes on even after a change. The King is dead, but looking at the bigger picture—a new King will take his place. This card is an important message to accept change.

Reversed- A change is still coming and as with death, you can't try to bargain. You might be scared of the change and so you try to avoid it. Burying your head in the sand could mean you aren't prepared for the change.

Temperance

Temperance has one foot in a river, in touch with her emotions, and the other is grounded. She is wearing a long white robe and has large red wings. She has a triangle on her chest and a circle on her forehead. She is pouring water from one cup to another. A path goes up through the middle of a field to the mountain where the Sun rises. Temperance wants you to focus on a path that doesn't take you to either extreme, neither too much of something nor not enough. This is how you will find the knowledge you need and peace.

Reversed- It is possible that this card is pointing to an imbalance or lack of harmony.

You should look at ways to fix this before trying to make other changes in your life. Don't get stuck in a situation where you do nothing, because you don't want to rock the boat.

The Devil

Like Death, we often jump to the wrong conclusion with this card. The Devil is half man, half goat, with the face of a lion and bat-like wings. You can also see an inverted pentagram above its head. There is a man and a woman in front of the devil. They are chained to the chair the Devil is perched on. They both have horns and tails, although the woman's tail has grapes and the man's tail has fire. Some may see this as signs of food and sex, or lust, two of our main desires. The Devil isn't trying to control the people. The black background is a reminder that we all have a dark side, but it's up to us to create balance, rather than ignore it.

Reversed- Don't assume it's a sign that you aren't lustful or passionate. In fact, it could be that you need to learn how to control your sexuality more. Relationships might be hard for you because of this.

The Tower

If you thought Death and the Devil were bad cards, the Tower will shock you. The images are shocking and this is the least favourite of all the tarot cards. The tall tower is situated on top of a mountain, which is falling away. It has been hit by lightning and the fire is causing people to fall from the higher windows. A rich man and a poor man are falling, a sign that nature knows no boundaries. Changes are coming and they will be disruptive, but can make way for a fresh start.

Reversed- You could probably be dealing with your problems in the wrong manner and it might even be making things worse. Even bad situations have something that we can learn.

The Star

The Star is refreshingly positive after the Tower. The bright blue sky has a large

eight-pointed star with seven smaller stars around it. There is a naked woman and, like Temperance, she has one foot in the water. She is pouring water from one of her jugs onto the land and new life is growing. I love this card, because the meaning is simple. If we have nothing to lose, there is nothing holding us back. If you share the little you have, you will be rewarded with more.

Reversed- You should feel more confident about your plans and decisions, maybe it would help if you listened to your instincts more. This will also help shift the feeling that you are stuck.

The Moon

The Moon has very similar colors to the Star. There is water, green land and a bright blue sky. The Star has been replaced with a Moon and the face is the Moon is looking down on the world. There are two towers with a very narrow path from a dog and a wolf leading to the middle of the towers. These animals represent our tame and wild sides. There is a crawfish leaving the water heading towards the dog and the wolf. Depending on your situation, you may be feeling brave or unaware of the danger that might be in front of you.

Reversed- If you are worried, nervous, or confused, you need to work through these feelings. Keep your feet on the ground because not being in touch with the real word may cause you more problems.

The Sun

It makes sense that the Sun is such a positive card: I know I feel better on a sunny day! Even the young boy riding the horse looks as if he is full of happiness. It seems like he is celebrating that he has made it over the wall behind him. On the wall, there are four sunflowers, all facing the boy. The boy is holding a large orange banner. This card often means you have succeeded in overcoming an obstacle. Your problems are behind you and you can look forward to some fun in life.

Reversed- If you are lacking confidence, you should know that trying new things can help. If your confidence is a little too high, remember that it may not last. Don't get trapped dwelling on the negative, because you might miss all the good in the world.

Judgement

All the people on Earth are ashen grey and looking up towards an angel in the sky. They are all naked and they have no possessions and are therefore equal. What has happened in their lives is now irrelevant. The angel has red and purple wings and blue clothes. He is wise, pure, and calm. His trumpet has a St. George's flag and it is traditionally a trumpet that sounds for announcements. This is a period of resurrection, reflection and new beginnings.

Reversed- There is probably a lot of self-doubt and you are possibly being too hard on yourself. It's likely that you are making the wrong decisions. Don't forget that your actions have consequences and at some point, you will have to face Judgement.

The World

The final card completes the cycle. A woman floats in the center of the card, the sky blue behind her. Her legs are facing the right, but she is looking to the left. She is surrounded by a green wreath with a red ribbon on top. More symbols include the angel's head, the ox, the eagle and the lion in the four corners. They represent the four Gospels, four of the zodiac signs and stability. You have reached a significant time in life and this cycle that you have completed has made you stronger and better.

Reversed- Quite literally, in the reverse, you may have things that are incomplete or that you have missed opportunities that were offered to you. Sometimes this is because of your own fear or doubts, but it could mean there is someone in your life who is preventing you from moving forward.

I have just touched on some of the images in the Major Arcana cards. Each card can have a different meaning for you, depending on your question. Just remember that these cards are more related to those bigger questions in life, so aim to look at the bigger picture.

THE CUPS SUIT

A spread that is dominated by cups is pointing to your emotions; perhaps there are conflicts that need to be resolved, matters of the heart. The cups are related to the element of water and I like to imagine our emotions being able to flow as water does. There may be relations with those who have a water zodiac sign—Pisces, Cancer, and Scorpio.

The Ace of Cups

One cup sits in the palm of a white hand that seems to be coming out of a cloud. Water flows out of the cup into a body of water below. Pay attention to the five streams of water leaving the cup and the twenty-five droplets. The white dove is carrying a Eucharist in its beak, maybe like it is going to drop it into the cup. There is a W on the cup, or it could be an M—woman or man. Lilies float in the water and there is green land in the distance. This card encourages you to use your imagination, instead of only looking from your own perspective.

Reversed- It's possible that you are hiding from your true feelings or struggling to express them. There might be someone in your life who can't control their emotional outbursts.

The Two of Cups

It's a happy scene between a man and a woman. It seems like a ceremony; it reminds me of when couples link arms to drink champagne on their wedding day. The woman wears blue and white, while the man is in yellow and black, a less frequent combination. This card is very much about the bond between two people, as there is nobody else in the card. Not only are there two cups but also two snakes and the lion head has two wings.

Reversed- Unfortunately, upturned often points to problems in a relationship. The disagreements might be so bad that if you don't make a change, there is little hope.

The Three of Cups

The Three of Cups is reminding us not to forget the groups and communities in our lives. Three women are dancing in a circle. Instead of the handbags in the center, the focus of the women is their raised cups, arms linked to show the closeness of their friendship. At this moment, the women have all they need to be happy, and that is each other and so you shouldn't be trying to achieve things alone.

Reversed- It could be that you are feeling lonely or that the dynamics of your group aren't quite right and you feel left out. Don't feel like you should change to fit in with the crowd.

The Four of Cups

We go back to solitude with the Four of Cups, but not in a bad way. A man is sitting under a tree, with crossed arms and legs. He looks like he is contemplating things and doesn't pay attention to the hand coming out of the cloud, offering him a cup. The other three cups are in a row in front of him. Often, this card points to missing out on opportunities, because we aren't able to look beyond ourselves. It's good to spend some time alone, but not so much that you aren't able to see the amazing things that are in front of you.

Reversed- Like the man, you might be ignoring emotional ties. You may have an emotional opportunity in front of you, but you need to make an effort to get it.

The Five of Cups

There is a bit of a darker scene with this card, both in colours and meaning. The sky is now grey and a woman wearing a long black robe has her head bowed low and her back to us. Three of the cups have been knocked over, and red and green liquid pours out of them, a sign of loss of life and magic. It indicates a loss of some kind or maybe a failure, but there is a great deal of pain as a result. The woman could refill the cups or cross the bridge to go home, but instead, she takes the time to grieve her loss.

Reversed- You have moved past this time of grief and it's time to start moving on. It's normal to still feel sad, but the other two cups are still upright, a sign that you should concentrate on them.

The Six of Cups

There is so much yellow in this card that you can instantly see a different tone to the Five of Cups. There is a boy offering a girl a cup with a white flower in it. There is another cup behind him and four more on the ground, all with a white flower in them. I like the mixture of innocence and purity, yet the children are in a city and there is a guard walking away from them, so there is still the need for protection. This card reminds us of the joy of children and the simple things in life, like having fun.

Reversed- Somebody may have a habit of crushing spirits, because they are so skeptical of everything. It can also suggest a childhood that wasn't quite so happy. Know that holding onto your past isn't healthy.

The Seven of Cups

The Seven of Cups is all about the choices that we have in front of us and how they can be rather intimidating at times. A man is facing seven cups in a cloud, although we can only see a silhouette of him. Each cup has a different symbol, a female head, a person covered in a white cloth, a snake, a dragon, a wreath, gems, and a tower. It's difficult to decide which is the right cup to choose because there could be positive and negative consequences with each.

Reversed- The choices you have aren't as varied as you think. You might be chasing a dream or perhaps doubting what it is that you really want.

The Eight of Cups

I have mixed feelings about this card. There are five stacked cups and another three in a different pile. The five represent sadness and the three happiness, so all is not lost. The Sun sits in the crescent of the Moon. The face shows no emotion. A man wearing red has crossed the river and has left the cups behind. He is about to start his new journey and it feels like he has accepted that he needs to leave the emotional baggage in his past.

Reversed- I feel a connection with the Seven of Cups. You might feel like you have made the wrong choice and you are trying to move forward the best you can. You may not be ready to start a new phase in life or just refusing to start.

The Nine of Cups

There is a man sitting with a semi-circle of nine cups behind him. He is wearing a white robe, yellow shoes and a red hat. He is happy and because the cups are about emotions, it's not material things that put the smile on his face. He doesn't keep his cups close to him or even look at them. He is happy to share because he isn't worried that his good fortune can be taken from him. He isn't a king, so he has had to work hard to get what he wanted, and so will you.

Reversed- You may well be missing something in your life or you haven't got what you wanted. You might be putting on a show trying to convince others of your happiness and success, but this comes at a cost, maybe even an obsession or addiction in other areas of your life.

The Ten of Cups

This is probably my favorite of the Cups suit. There is a huge rainbow with ten cups in it. The rainbow shines over the roof of a house, a river, a sandy beach and a family. The man holds the woman around the waist as they reach up to the sky. The children are happily playing nearby. The family have received good fortune, dreams have come true and they are grateful for this. They have had their difficult times but everything turned out all right.

Reversed- You may have had a string of bad luck and or your idea of success is slightly off and it's impossible to feel happy. Start looking at the smaller things in life to find happiness.

The Page of Cups

A rather elegant-looking man dressed in blue and pink is standing on a sandy beach with the water behind him. The cup is in his right hand but more interestingly, there is a blue fish inside the cup. It even looks as if the two are having a conversation. The fish is a symbol of new beginnings, creativity and imagination. Listening to the fish is like listening to the inspiration that pops up in us every now and again.

Reversed- More often than not, in this position, you are lacking creativity or you are using it for things that you shouldn't. It's important that you concentrate your efforts in turning the dream into a reality.

The Knight of Cups

The knight in shining armor riding a white horse is a cliché, but there is a lot more detail t0 this image. First of all, he is the most romantic of the four knights; the red fish on his cloak shows his creativity and passion. But the wings on his helmet and boots point to his connection to the spiritual world. The land around him is dry, with just a river in his path. Perhaps in preparation for his long journey, he is going to fill up his cup.

Reversed- Take care not to ignore the feelings of others because you are wrapped up in your emotions. You may feel like you need to be more creative or it's possible that you have some imaginative impulses that are making you uncomfortable.

The Queen of Cups

The Queen sits on a throne that might be on an island. Her throne is engraved with cherubs, another connection to children, angels, and the higher world. She is wearing blue and white and she holds her cup in her hand. The cup isn't the same as the other cups. Maybe I am a little too imaginative, but it looks like a little robot. The point is that the cub has a lid. It is mysterious and maybe she wants to keep a lid on her thoughts and feelings. The Queen looks at her cup lovingly and will love and help those around her.

Reversed- Sometimes, this position points to someone who isn't in control of their feelings or their imagination. Other times it shows a person who struggles to understand other people's emotions, this may cause problems like manipulation and emotional vacuums in relationships.

The King of Cups

For a court card, it's not as royal as you would think. The King sits on a throne that is in the middle of a rough sea. The ship and the fish are being thrown around. He is wearing a blue robe and a yellow cloak with red trimmings. He has a cup in one hand and a scepter in the other. He is not bothered by the rough waters around him; in fact, he seems quite calm. One foot is close to the water. He doesn't fear his emotions; quite the reverse, he is in control of them. He is thoughtful and will listen to the thoughts and opinions of others before making a decision.

Reversed- Remember the importance of boundaries and not getting your feelings confused with those of others. This could be a sign that you need to increase your emotional intelligence so that you are better at coping with other people's emotions.

So, the main theme that runs through the Cups suit is our emotions and learning to find balance in expressing them. Our imagination and creativity are also important. The strongest colour throughout the cards is blue and we can see this with both the clothes and the water. There are other smaller details, like the wings and angels, that remind us of the importance of spirituality.

THE PENTACLES SUIT

These fourteen cards look at the day-to-day parts of our lives, such as our health, career and financial situation. On a deeper level, they can explain more about our self-esteem and how we view ourselves. The Pentacles are associated with the earth element, being grounded and our own growth. The Pentacles can give insights into those in our life who are earth signs, like Taurus, Virgo and Capricorn.

The Ace of Pentacles

As with the Ace of Cups, we see another hand appearing from a cloud with a pentacle cupped in it. The hand is white while the cloud blends in with the blue sky. The pentacle looks like it could be the Sun and even the hand shines brightly. There is a path between green fields and it leads to bushes with an archway. The pentacle could be leading the way to something better on the other side. You should think about what you can hold in your hands and what this will enable you to achieve.

Reversed- In the upturned position, you might have missed opportunities or turned a blind eye to small opportunities that you thought weren't worth it. Don't underestimate the value of money.

The Two of Pentacles

It's the ridiculous-looking hat the man is wearing that you may spot first. This is loosely related to the ships on the rough waves behind the man. Regardless of the troubles behind him or what others think of him, his concentration remains on keeping his pentacles balanced. His clothes are red and orange, meaning magic and enthusiasm. The green infinity loop around the pentacles is a sign of life. If he can maintain control over his pentacles, he can stay happy.

Reversed- There could be some imbalance in your life, financially, career, home life, or even your emotions. Rather than worrying what others think of you, take some time to figure out how to get more control again.

The Three of Pentacles

There is something about this card that reminds me of a Ken Follett book. A young man is standing on a bench working on a cathedral arch. The three pentacles are at the top of the arch. He is talking to a monk and perhaps an architect as he has plans in his hands. There is a balance between wisdom, age and skill. If you draw this card, it shows that you may need to listen to others if you want to create something amazing.

Reversed- The warning here is "more haste, less speed". If you go at things too quickly, you are unlikely to succeed. You should also listen to the advice of those who know more. If you feel like people don't listen to your advice, you need to work on your confidence.

The Four of Pentacles

This is another card full of balance and control. A man is sitting on a stone in front of a colourful city. He has one pentacle on his head, another between his arms and one under each foot. It's hard to tell if the man is taking control of the pentacles or if they are preventing him from going anywhere. It's clear that he doesn't want to share his wealth, but this doesn't make him greedy. It may suggest that he is more concerned about material possessions than he should be.

Reversed- Money can't buy happiness and it shouldn't be more important than your loved ones. If you aren't that well off financially, it doesn't mean that you aren't fortunate, and at the same time, don't overestimate what wealth you do have.

The Five of Pentacles

Until now, we have seen images of people managing their wealth, but the Five of Pentacles has two poor people struggling through the snow. What's more, the man is on crutches. They are wearing the right colour clothes—blue, green, orange and red—but they are torn. The five pentacles are in a stained-glass window, maybe a church. They almost look like they are in the form of a tree. Without wealth, life is hard, but there is help, if the couple chooses to go inside the church.

Reversed- You have probably gone through the worst of your hard times and although it's not quite over, there is light at the end of the tunnel. If you are becoming more financially stable, you can learn to be a little more relaxed with your spending.

The Six of Pentacles

The couple on the floor are dressed the same way as the couple in the Five of Pentacles, but there is no snow and they have learnt how to ask for help. A man is giving them coins, but in his other hand, he holds scales. The six pentacles are in the sky around him, however, they aren't balanced. This card isn't necessary about balance, but more about appreciating the fact that not everyone is equal.

Reversed- You may be working incredibly hard, but someone else is spending your money. This could lead you not to trust this person and stop being so generous. It could also mean you are gaining wealth but a loved one is losing it.

The Seven of Pentacles

I find this quite a reassuring card. There is a man looking over his grape vines. Maybe he is watching them grow or maybe he is trying to decide if it is the right time to harvest the grapes. The pentacles are on the grape vines. One pentacle is one the ground, perhaps a sign that they are almost ready. This card is all about patience. He has his tool, he has worked hard and things are growing. Now it's about waiting for the right moment.

Reversed- It is quite the opposite when upturned—a lack of patience or hard work. Instead of focusing on one thing, you might be trying to juggle too many and you aren't seeing the rewards.

The Eight of Pentacles

A carpenter is working on a pentacle. Six are already placed on a tree and the eighth is on the ground, ready to be put up next. His blue shirt suggests he is calm, while his red stockings imply he is passionate about his work. He is alone, but this only enables him to focus more. We don't know if he will keep the pentacles or give them to someone. The point is that he is making an effort and he takes pride in his work. It may also mean that you need to keep perfecting your skills until you get your work right.

Reversed- Watch out for becoming a perfectionist: you may end up going overboard and destroying your hard work. In this position, it might suggest that you need to work on developing your skills.

The Nine of Pentacles

This time, we see a woman with the pentacles on grapevines. This difference is, the man only had one bush, whereas the woman has a field full of ripe grapes, a sign of plenty. The falcon on her hand points to her complete control and because of her control, she is able to create so much. She is happy, and for the time being, she can enjoy her rewards. But a tiny snail is moving towards her crop. It has the ability to destroy it, so remember that nothing lasts forever.

Reversed- You can't wait for others to provide you with wealth or you need a little more self-control to succeed. Enjoy everything you have right now rather than concerning yourself too much about the future.

The Ten of Pentacles

My OCD kicks in a little with this card. There is an awful lot happening and there seems to be tons of imagery. Plus, the pentacles are just on the card, not randomly placed (look for the shape of the Kabbalah Tree of Life) but almost like they are stickers you want to peel off to see what's underneath. Probably the most significant symbol is the old man watching his family. He has worked for his wealth and you can see this by his extravagant cloak. Now it is time to sit back and enjoy his family. His faithful dogs look up to him respectfully.

Reversed- You haven't found the stability in life you are hoping for. There could be problems with your wealth because of your family or your business/career. It may also indicate that someone doesn't want to pass the baton on to the next person, whether that's in terms of knowledge or wealth.

The Page of Pentacles

A young man stands in a green field with a forest in the distance. To his left, there is bare land, ready for him to sow his seeds and plant his dreams. Behind the care field, you can see a mountain, a symbol of stability. He is holding his pentacle high, perhaps planning his fortune. The sky is the same colour as the pentacle, a good sign that fortune surrounds him. This card shows all the signs of new life. The man is young, but that doesn't mean that he can't achieve his dreams, as long as he stays focused.

Reversed- This is a strong indicator that you are being impractical, that your goals are too high or you don't have the confidence to achieve them. Don't allow yourself to take the easy road, or feel defeated when faced with obstacles.

The Knight of Pentacles

The Knight of Pentacles shows the next step after the Page. The fields have been ploughed and the dream is becoming a reality. The Knight of Pentacles still has to work hard to take care of them, but his black horse shows that he is serious about his work. The horse has a sprig of oak on the front of his head, a sign of courage. Both knight and horse stand determined, maybe even stubborn to succeed. The choices have been made and now it is a case of sticking to them.

Reversed- You need to find the motivation or courage to take the first steps. You might not be ready for the hard work ahead of you. If people around you don't share your enthusiasm, don't be disappointed.

The Queen of Pentacles

There are similarities with the Queen of Cups, but instead of the water, the Queen of Pentacles is surrounded by land and flowers. She also holds the pentacle a little more lovingly, almost maternally. Like with the page and the knight, the pentacle is the same colour as the sky. The red roses growing match her red robe. She has everything that she wanted and feels stable within her own life. Now she is dedicated to caring for something else.

Reversed- This is about not being in the right position to care for someone else or for the responsibilities that come with being an adult. You may also feel like you are giving so much, but not receiving an equal amount.

The King of Pentacles

The King's robe blends into the flowers that are growing all around him. He is sitting on a black throne, a connection maybe to the knight's black horse. The castle behind him emphasises his wealth. There are two gold oxen on his throne, a sign of his stubbornness. The pentacle rests on his knee. His armour shows that he is an active king. He has worked, he has practiced control and now he can enjoy his wealth. The same is available to you, if you work hard like the king and remain humble.

Reversed- it is possible that you are acting like the king but you haven't behaved in the same way. Look for solutions to your problems and don't let fear or pride get the better of you.

While the general theme of the Pentacles suit is money, I think that when you start to relate the various images, it goes beyond what's in your bank account. This suit is about our ambitions and in a few readings, I have got the sense that the cards reinforced a goal I had, but encouraged me and even helped me to see if I needed to work on my abilities or my self-esteem. It's also a good suit to remind us that sharing, helping, and giving to others is an important part of our journey.

THE SWORDS SUIT

In this chapter, we are going to take a closer look at the mind, thoughts and beliefs and the balance between intellect and power. There is a lot of action associated with the Swords and this action can be used for either good or bad. Because the Swords are linked to the element of air, they reflect Aquarians, Libras and Geminis.

The Ace of Swords

Our hand is back, holding a sword that points straight up. Unlike the other clouds that the hand appears from, this cloud is darker than the sky. There is a crown around the top of the sword and laurel leaves hang from the crown. The crown isn't held in place. Only the tip of the sword goes through the crown, highlighting the sharpness of the mind. The hand could be offering the sword or it could be challenging someone to take it. If you choose to take it, you hold the power to create or destroy. Your journey should include the search for truth.

Reversed- You might find it hard to clearly visualise your goals. You are intelligent but you may not be using it in the right way. Organise your opinions so that you have the confidence to share them.

The Two of Swords

Despite the two swords, I still feel that the images are quite calming. There is a woman dressed in white with yellow shoes, she is sitting on a white stone and the ground is also white. The blue water is separated from the sky by just a small amount of raised land. Only the Moon is in the sky. She has a sword in each hand, her arms are crossed and she is blindfolded. She has a decision to make but she has to rely on her intellect and intuition.

Reversed- The decision you need to make will be harder because all the information isn't available. If you feel you aren't brave enough to make the right decision, have faith in your intelligence.

The Three of Swords

It's true that this is not a good card, but remember that tarot guides only provide insight: they don't determine your future. There is a heart in the grey sky, and it's raining. The three swords are going straight through the heart. This card points to loss, possibly a death, or maybe it's the knowing that you won't be able to achieve your goals. It's hard to know what to do next when there is so much sadness.

Reversed- Unfortunately, there is still a lot of sadness, but reversed would indicate that you don't want to accept the situation. You keep going over your memories and it's probably going to leave you feeling exhausted.

The Four of Swords

After the Three of Swords, you might be nervous about the tomb in this card. The tomb is of a man, it's gold and there is a sword on the side. The other three swords are on the wall, but look as if they could hurt him if they fell. There is a stained-glass window, perhaps happy memories of his past. This card isn't about death, it's about taking a moment to be alone, step back and process what your mind is telling you, learn what you actually want before moving forward.

Reversed- Your mind is working overtime, which makes it difficult to take the break you need. Others won't leave you in peace to think. You might even be scared of what you find out if you take time to process your thoughts.

The Five of Swords

There are three men, one wearing green, red and orange, and the other two yellow. The man in green holds three swords, the other two are lying on the ground in front of the other men, who are walking away. The smile on the man's face suggests he has won this battle. The irony is, what can he do with three swords when he only has two hands? The other men are still alive, so the battle has more likely hurt their pride or social standing. The message here is that even if you are stronger and smarter than others, you can't risk pushing them out of your life.

Reversed- As with the double-edge of all the swords, winning this battle might mean that you have lost another —or even the metaphorical war. Perhaps you have reached a point where you don't want to be alone.

The Six of Swords

It's another card that is a little bleak. Even the water isn't blue, but rather an icy grey. There is a man paddling a boat with a woman and child sitting in front of him. We can't see their faces. The six swords are stood upright in front of the boat, but they haven't caused a leak. To the left, the water is calm, to the right it's rough, hinting at mixed emotions. The family has no possessions and we can't see what is ahead of the boat, but they know they need action to move forward.

Reversed- The only way is forward, but you are reluctant; maybe you even have a slight hope of going back to how things were. It's also possible that there are things preventing you from moving forward.

The Seven of Swords

The Seven of Swords is brighter and even a little amusing. There is a man with five swords in his arms. He is either running or maybe tiptoeing. There are two swords behind him. It's hard to tell if he is looking back at the swords he has left behind or the camp he has left. He hasn't spotted the three soldiers in the distance, so perhaps he hasn't completely escaped. This card shows determination, perhaps betrayal, selfishness and that you shouldn't be too quick to assume you have gotten away with things.

Reversed- There might be some disagreements ahead of you and the outcome may not be positive. Watch out for passive-aggressive behaviour, creating drama so that people can see you aren't happy.

The Eight of Swords

We are back to the grey sky with the Eight of Swords. A woman is tied up and blindfolded. The eight swords look like a fence behind her, but she isn't tied to them. Although there is water under her, her feet aren't touching it, implying her problems aren't related to her feelings. It's obvious that the woman is restricted in her choices, but if she wants to break free, she will touch the water and therefore her emotions. Her mind might be blocked but her legs are still free. We shouldn't always rely on our intelligence to solve problems.

Reversed- In this position, it's likely that you've been through a situation where you needed something other than your intelligence. You may have tried something and it didn't work out as you had hoped. Don't be scared to try again.

The Nine of Swords

Our first thought is of the woman who is sitting upright in her bed as if she has had a bad dream. The swords are lined up behind her, but you can't tell if they are in the black sky or they are hanging on a black wall. There is a lot of symbolism if you look closely: the blanket is covered in roses and astrological signs, the bed has carvings of a fight. Her pillow is yellow. Still, the main point is the nightmare, the fears we can't control.

Reversed- One meaning could be that you now understand what you are scared of or what is troubling you. Alternatively, your negative emotions are so overwhelming that you can't get out of your distress.

The Ten of Swords

Again, not the most positive-looking card. There is a man on the ground, the ten swords stabbing him from his head to the base of his spine, and there is a red cloth draped over him. The mountains are blue and the yellow sky is being overtaken by the black clouds. The worst really has happened and this is the end of the tragedy. Whatever you have been doing mentally hasn't been working and it's time to make a change.

Reversed- The worst has still happened but you are not facing this. Try not to waste your energy fixing something that can't be fixed and remember that you need to move on from the suffering instead of getting stuck there.

The Page of Swords

We are back to a positive image with the Page of Swords. A young man stands on a hill, the wind in his hair and his sword held up ready for action. He may have had to fight to get to where he is or maybe he is ready to defend his position. This position on top of the hill is an advantageous one. His yellow clothes show his intelligence and his red boots, passion. This card represents the creation of thoughts and new ideas. It represents honesty and searching for justice. The page will need courage for his journey, through the wind and to find the truth.

Reversed- You may need to work on your mind to develop your thoughts. If you can learn new things, you will see a great improvement in your self-esteem and stop feeling like you don't match up to others.

The Knight of Swords

The knight is full of action and it's motivating. His horse is at full speed and he holds his sword high in the air. He is full of courage and nothing is going to stop him. The knight passes the same windblown tree that was behind the Page of Swords. The knight has his idea and he is determined to see it through. This card is telling you that if you want a change or something new, you will need the same enthusiasm and drive as the knight.

Reversed- You might have the idea but you need to be focused more to take the first step. You are lacking the bravery that the knight has, or perhaps you listen too much to people who don't believe in your abilities.

The Queen of Swords

The Queen of Swords is different to the other queens. There are no flowers or greenery growing and she doesn't look at her sword lovingly. The queen sits on a throne, and her hand is raised as if she is addressing the crowd. The throne is white, so are her robes. There are clouds behind her, making her look like a goddess. The river behind her implies her decisions aren't affected by her emotions. She relies on her own intelligence and people respect her for this. If you draw this card, you should find the same confidence the queen has.

Reversed- In this position it might be a sign that you find it easier to follow others than make you own choices. You might not always be honest and perhaps put your foot in it at times.

The King of Swords

It's almost like we are looking at a front-on version of the queen. The king is sitting on his throne with his sword in the same hand and same position as the queen. The angel in his crown shows his connection to the divine. He is intelligent and fair, but he also looks quite stern. He doesn't put up with people who are going to waste his time. He is aware that he needs to set the right example. Like the queen, he will not consider emotions when making choices. He will look at all perspectives to make decisions.

Reversed- It might be possible that you are using your intelligence for the wrong reasons. Unlike the stern king, you take the rules so seriously that you may appear a little bullyish.

There are a lot of ups and downs with the Swords suit. There is some amazing imagery that inspires and makes you want to get up and create new plans. There are also quite a few dark cards, but I think it's so important not to jump to the wrong conclusions. I know how easy it is to assume the worst, instead of taking a moment to look closer at the symbols and messages and relate them back to your questions. I suppose the whole point of the Swords suit is to use your intelligence over emotions and this applies to the positive and the negative cards.

THE WANDS SUIT

The wands are all about what makes us who we are, our consciousness, our ego, and our energy. They give us insight into our strengths and ambitions, as well as highlighting our intuition and even our sexuality, which makes sense, as they are linked to the element of fire. This suit can represent the fire zodiac signs—Leo, Sagittarius and Aries.

The Ace of Wands

Our familiar white hand appears from a large gray cloud holding a wand. New leaves are sprouting from the wand and the scene below is inviting. There is a river flowing through green fields. There are mountains and maybe a castle in the background. The river separates the hand from the mountains. The wand is an offering, an offering of a new beginning that is different from the path that others are on.

Reversed- Even though you know the right thing to do is start afresh, you are worried about this because you are going to have to overcome your fear of doing new things. You might not feel you have the time or the knowledge but don't listen to these excuses.

The Two of Wands

A man holds one wand in his hand and another stands upright next to him. He is standing at the top of what looks like a castle and I like to think it's the castle in the Ace of Wands, because there is also a green field and a river. The man has a globe in his other hand. What might be more important are the roses and lilies below the wand, the balance between passion and purity or between our determination and letting things go. This card wants us to think of the plan behind the action we are about to take.

Reversed- Try not to rush things and end up making mistakes, but then don't go to the other extreme where you are trying harder than necessary and it takes longer. Even reversed, this card points to balance.

The Three of Wands

The sky is bright gold and so is the land, but there isn't the same growth as before. A man stands overlooking the dry land, one wand is to his left and the other two to the right. The road ahead seems more positive than with the previous wands, there are no ships fighting the waves and although this man doesn't hold the globe; the future's still bright. If you draw this card, it's a good sign to keep going, because what lies ahead is positive.

Reversed- You know your plan, but you may lack the courage to start. It is also possible that you have started a new journey, even though you aren't completely sure where you are going. Even if you aren't happy about this new direction, know that you are heading the right way.

The Four of Wands

This is a lovely card: the sky is still bright and the four wands are draped with a canopy, inviting you to the celebration. The couple might be celebrating their wedding; there are a few guests there already. The large castle in the background represents purity and stability. It's a sign of places and people that make you feel welcome. The wed couple has made the decision to be happy; you should do the same.

Reversed- Maybe you can't find peace or you don't feel welcome in certain situations. You might feel like your life is unstable because of some problems you have with people.

The Five of Wands

I always feel like there is such a huge contrast with the previous card, but not necessarily in a bad way. First, the sky is bright blue. Second, there are five men, each with a wand. It might be a fight or a game, but it's important that each man is using his wand in a different way. If they are trying to work together, it's obviously not working. This new group of people have a goal or a mission, but it suggests the first steps towards becoming organised isn't always easy.

Reversed- If you find it hard to work with a particular group, it could be because you can't concentrate or you aren't happy with the group dynamics. You might be tempted to go it alone, but if you can stay patient, you can benefit from the group once it becomes stronger.

The Six of Wands

We have lots of great colours in this card. The white horse covered in a green cloak, the man riding the horse has a red robe with a touch of yellow underneath and orange trousers. Five men to his side carry their wands, the man holding the sixth with a wreath on the top and another on his head. This man seems to have successfully organised the chaotic group of men and is now being praised for his success. If you have achieved something and are reaping the rewards, remember that it may or may not last.

Reversed- It can indicate that someone is overly arrogant about their achievements or that they are expecting recognition for something they haven't done. If this isn't you, be careful that your humility doesn't let others take advantage of you.

The Seven of Wands

The man looks as if he has been working hard to create a barrier with six wands and he is ready to place the seventh. Whatever the man achieved in the Six of Wands, this man is determined to protect. By his position, he doesn't seem to have much choice. What I love about this card is how he is balanced over a small stream, yet he is wearing odd shoes—a sign that he is confident, but that there is still part of him that is cautious. Consider all of the things you have that need protecting, even things like your reputation.

Reversed- It's likely that there have been times that you didn't defend yourself, either because you couldn't or it was easier not to. Try not to rely too much on what others think or to be too sensitive to what others think.

Eight of Wands

Like the Seven of Wands, there is a bright blue sky and green land. This is one of the few cards that doesn't have any people. There are just eight wands, parallel in the sky. We aren't sure if they are all moving down to the ground or up to the sky, but they are able to move in any direction they wish. The freedom of the wands is what we need to learn from. This card is a sign that we need to get rid of all that weighs us down so that we can be free.

Reversed- It's hard to find the right pace. You may not have the same enthusiasm to move forward as the wands do and your journey is taking too long. If you feel the opposite and things are all rushed, take a moment to enjoy the beauty in life.

Nine of Wands

The man now stands in front of eight wands as he leans on the ninth for support. He has a bandage around his head. The man looks suspicious, perhaps concerned about what the wands can do. It might be that the man is paranoid, because nobody on the card is out to get him. The bandage might be a sign of his hurt pride; the colours of his clothes suggest he has plenty to be happy about, so it might be emotional. If you receive this card, it is a sign that you may have challenges ahead, but you will be able to keep going.

Reversed- You need to find more courage so that you can face all of your problems. However, you might not see this, because you are too busy blaming others for your problems.

Ten of Wands

This man has scooped up his ten wands and is carrying them towards a village. It's hard work, but he keeps his head down and continues. His orange and brown clothes represent enthusiasm and strength, so we know he will make it with that last bit of effort. The Ten of Wands is a sign of the finish line and that your efforts will soon pay off. The last leg of this race points to success after all of your ups and downs. It might have taken more effort than others had to make, but there is no need to feel bad about this.

Reversed- The weight of the wands might be heavier than necessary, because you are carrying an additional burden. There may be too much self-pity or looking for approval from others. If the burden you carry isn't yours, it's time to get rid of it.

The Page of Wands

This card makes me smile. Maybe it's the white hat, or maybe it's the confidence the Page of Wands has. He is looking at his wand like it's the first time he has seen it and it seems like it's the source of his inspiration. He is alone, but this doesn't bother him, because he is so happy with his wand. The colours of his clothes are a mixture of innocence, magic, the higher mind and passion. His tunic is covered with salamanders. If you receive this card, it means you should be happy about going about things alone. It's time to make a new, unique path for yourself.

Reversed- The fear of being alone could be blocking your creativity or you might be being too hard on yourself. Although you don't know what is in front of you, know that repeating the same thing isn't going to help.

The Knight of Wands

The Knight of Wands is riding a brown horse rearing up ready for action. The knight is in a full suit of body armour and a yellow tunic with salamanders. The tunic is torn, maybe from the battle or maybe from trying to get it over his armour. We can't see what is ahead of the knight, but he is riding away from three pyramids or mountains, the challenges he has overcome. The Page of Wands had a dream and the Knight of Wands has the confidence to carry out the dreams. That being said, the knight is quite young. He may not have the knowledge or skill, or he may even be a little too confident for what lays ahead.

Reversed- You have skill, but you might be overestimating the level of your skills. You may be impulsive and need to take more time to think about the plan and the outcomes. In some cases, you may not have enough confidence and you are too scared to move forward.

The Queen of Wands

In one hand, the queen holds her wand, in the other, a sunflower. She sits in her throne decorated with lions, and she is wearing a yellow robe and a white cloak, a contradiction to the black cat at her feet. The cat looks straight at us, but the queen looks to one side. The queen seems to have it all—intelligence, beauty, sexuality, and a dark side. The subtleness of her toe pointing out from her robe shows that she is involved in all. This is a very powerful and feminine card to receive, a symbol of your own confidence.

Reversed- It may be hard for you to see your femininity or your confidence to get things done. Those around you might not appreciate who you truly are. Try not to let things get on top of you because you fear your own potential.

. . .

The King of Wands

You will notice a lot of salamanders in this card, on the king's throne, cloak and one at his feet. His red hair and robe point to the fire and passion of this man. You can also see lions on his throne, reminding us he is a brave man. The king looks into the distance; he is focused and not concerned about what is happening around him. His green shoes show that he isn't a dreamer and in fact is very much in touch with the real world. The way he holds his wand indicates that he is prepared and determined. Whether it's a battle or his goals, he is ready to succeed.

Reversed- You probably have a lot of ambitions, but you may not have the skills to fulfill them. The other possibility is that you have too much confidence in your skills and this is making you come across as a bit of a brag. If you are acting like a bully, it is probably a sign that you are being bullied.

Please remember that this is a guide and for a successful reading, you need to use your intuition as well. What you will probably find is that this book is a great reference to get you started while you build up your confidence and knowledge of the symbols, colours and meanings. After some time, you will get better at seeing the relationship between a card and your situations.

CONCLUSION

That's it! You now have all the knowledge you need to start reading your own tarot cards. If you haven't already, now is the time to get yourself a deck and give them a good shuffle. My advice would be to get yourself a Rider Waite to start off with. It is such a nice deck for learners and it sounds weird, but the cards feel comfortable in your hands. Maybe it's because they are the most familiar images that they are easier to relate to. Once you are into the swing of things, your familiarity with the images will make it easier to recognise the same imagery in other decks.

After going back through the rich history of the tarot cards, it's now difficult to associate them with dark, mysterious corner stores or online scams. Hopefully, I have cleared up the myths of predicting the future. The cards aren't going to tell you about your future love or whether or not you are going to win the lottery.

Now, you can use tarot cards to help you understand parts of your past, present and future. The insights that you gain can assist you in making decisions that will lead you down a better path. But nothing is ever set in stone. Never forget that these insights aren't guaranteed. Let's say that you have two career paths and the cards seem to point in favour of one over the other. It's still down to you to make that final decision. With this in mind, it's also not right to blame the cards when things don't go your way. Our destiny is always in our own hands.

It's been a rather emotional rollercoaster for me. Even after quite a few years of doing my own readings, it was a great experience to delve into the intricate details of each element, suit, and card. It also allowed me to get out some of my earlier journals and see the progress in my understanding and even how my questions have advanced. I recommend that you keep a journal as well. It's not as though the only thing we have on our minds is the next reading. As you can now see, with so much potential information, it is impossible to remember everything.

You should also use your journal to jot down any questions that come to mind before you start your reading. So often, I am driving or plodding around the supermarket and a question pops up. Not like what I want for dinner that night, but you know how your brain works!

We have also learnt of some other skills that you may have thought didn't have much relation to tarot cards. Again, I hope I have revamped the image of the teenage witch from the 90s into something more realistic and practical. Many of the techniques we looked at can be transferred to other areas of spiritualism. For example, the protection circle we create when making a spell can also be used to enhance meditation. Even in Buddhism, the protection mandala can help meditation, or creating a circle with your thumb and index finger forms a circle, a familiar symbol in feng shui. Pay close attention to the power of circles!

Another thing that I think you should bear in mind is that not every card will always have significance. A mistake I made in the beginning, which I admit made me look a bit like a crazy scientist on a whiteboard, was to be convinced I was missing something. You can see that this was probably just a lack of confidence in understanding the meanings of the cards. But I would read through books and books trying to find what I was missing. If you don't see a meaning or relate to a card, it's perfectly normal, so don't feel like you are doing anything wrong.

When this happens to me, I take note of the images and symbols in the card, just a short message to myself on my phone. The days after drawing a card that seems to have no relevance, I keep my eyes open for related symbols. An unexpected rainbow, a lion carved into a stone, and especially any signs of cups, swords, wands or pentacles. You may not see the relationship straight away, but you will be surprised when the penny drops.

This is the fun side of tarot cards— the synchronicity. You can walk through your entire life and miss these connected events or symbols. The black cat in the Queen of Wands is a classic example. Black cats are associated with black magic and bad luck. Now I see a black cat and I wonder why I am being reminded of my darker side. On a similar note, don't forget not to jump to those wrong conclusions when you see a strong card like the Hanged Man or Death. The Fool isn't an idiot and the Wheel of Fortune doesn't automatically imply you are in for good things. If you are a beginner, try to erase any stereotypical ideas you have of the cards before you start. It will help you to begin reading the cards in a more efficient manner.

Give yourself enough time for a reading—time and a deck of cards is all you need. Yes, you can buy candles, crystals and essential oils. You can set the scene, if you think it will help, but time is crucial. If you rush through, you won't have enough time to find the answers to these difficult questions. The other thing you may find is that because you rush, you feel the need to have another reading before time has passed to make sense of the first reading. Rushing anything takes the fun out of it, and the last thing to remember is that it should, above everything, be enjoyable.

If you are new to my books, I thank you from the bottom of my heart for choosing to read this combination of years of research and practice. If you have read *Healing Mantras* and/or *Modern Chakras*, I hope this has been as practical as the others and that like me, you can appreciate a more spiritual living and overall, a happier life. Join me on Facebook and you can contact me on my website too. Of course, I will be forever grateful if you could take a minute to leave your feedback on Amazon so I can continue my learning journey while I prepare for the next book! Good luck and I would love to hear how your readings are going.

Thank you for reading my book. If you have enjoyed reading it perhaps you would like to leave a star rating and a review for me on Amazon? It really helps support writers like myself create more books. You can leave a review for me by scanning the QR code below with your phone camera:

Thank you so much. Verda Harper

REFERENCES

Baikie, K. A. (2018, January 2). *Emotional and physical health benefits of expressive writing | Advances in Psychiatric Treatment*. Cambridge Core. https://www.cambridge.org/core/journals/ advances-in-psychiatric-treatment/article/emotional-and-physical-health-benefits-of-expressive-writing/ED2976A61F5DE56B46F07A1CE9EA9F9F

Burroughs Cook, A. (2009). *What falls to the Floor...* tarot Dynamics. http://tarotdynamicsannacook.blogspot.com/p/what-falls-to-floor.html

Categories: tarot Readings. (n.d.). Psychic Reviews. https://www.psychicreviews.com/guides-expanded/tarot-readings/

Dore, J. (2017, September 2). *Using tarot in Psychotherapy.* Psych Central. https://www.psychcentral.com/pro/using-tarot-in-psychotherapy#1

Douglas, C. (ed) (1997) *Visions: Notes of the Seminar given in 1930-1934 by C. G. Jung.* Vol. 2. p 923. Princeton University Press.

Hammond, C. (2017, June 2). *The puzzling way that writing heals the body.* BBC Future. https://www.bbc.com/future/article/20170601-can-writing-about-pain-make-you-heal-faster

Hancock, P. (n.d.). *tarot Spreads.* Psychic Revelation. https://www.psychic-revelation.com/reference/q_t/tarot/tarot_spreads/

Jones, J. (2017, September 1). *Carl Jung: tarot Cards Provide Doorways to the Unconscious, and Maybe a Way to Predict the Future.* Open Culture. https://www.openculture.com/2017/08/carl-jung-tarot-cards-provide-doorways-to-the-unconscious-and-even-a-way-to-predict-the-future.html

Labyrinthos Academy. (2017, February 26). *tarot and Numerology: What do numbers in tarot Mean for the Minor Arcana? (Infographic).* Labyrinthos. https://labyrinthos.co/blogs/learn-tarot-with -labyrinthos-academy/tarot-and-numerology- what-do-numbers-in-tarot-mean-for-the-minor- arcana-infographic

Michelsen, T. (n.d.). *Colour Meanings on tarot Cards – tarot Moon.* tarot Moon. https://tarotmoon.com/colour-meanings-on-tarot-cards/

Moon Phases for Doing Spells. (n.d.). Free Witchcraft Spells. https://www.free-witchcraft-spells.com/moon-phases.html

Nguyen, T. (2017, December 6). *10 Surprising Benefits You'll Get From Keeping a Journal.* Huffpost.Com. https://www.huffpost.com/entry/benefits-of-journaling-_b_6648884?guccounter=1&guce_referrer=aHR0cHM6Ly93d3cu-Z29vZ2xlLmNvbS8&guce_referrer_sig=AQAAAN2lp-R5KmOyO-ezRS1AelU7zVREqNoIWSwr1Tgt30IkEq-pdy-D5xgUugI_Cs7JtymaMifLOLkjGtQAyb1Nvee H1qx39daqsQTRWHIJ0du-l6valHQ_ wFVjGskXjzUCB-IFSoIxqsVfzl6g5xu6vR 14gxAwvLIkAofqynYZG4tz0y

Oatman-Stanford, H. (2015, December 4). *tarot Mythology: The Surprising Origins of the World's Most Misunderstood Cards.* Mental Floss. https://www.mentalfloss.com/article/71927/tarot-mythology-surprising-origins-worlds-most-misunderstood-cards

Parry, M. (2020, January 17). *3 Self-Care Benefits Everyone Can Get from a Daily tarot Pull.* Brit + Co. https://www.brit.co/self-care-tarot-reading/

Patterson, R. (2018, May 11). *StackPath.* John Hunt Publishing. https://www.johnhuntpublishing.com/blogs/moon-books/tarot-spells/

Posada, J. (2007). *What is an Oracle?* Jenniferposada.Com. https://www.jenniferposada.com/what-is-an-oracle

Reed, T. (2019, December 18). *What are significators in a tarot reading?* The tarot Lady. https://www.thetarotlady.com/significators-tarot-reading/

Roos, M. (2019, November 6). *How to Connect tarot and Chakras*. Siobhan Johnson. https://www.siobhanjohnson.com/connect-tarot-chakras/

Sol, M. (2020, December 30). *Synchronicity: 7 Ways to Interpret and Manifest It ·*. LonerWolf. https://lonerwolf.com/synchronicity/

Staff, J. (2016, December 29). *tarot-Kabbalah connection not all that mysterious*. J.Weekly.Com. https://www.jweekly.com/2004/11/05/tarot-kabbalah-connection-not-all-that-mysterious/

tarot Card Meanings List - 78 Cards By Suit, Element, and Zodiac. (n.d.). Labyrinthos. https://labyrinthos.co/blogs/tarot-card-meanings-list

Whitehurst, T. (2020, August 13). *How to Cast a Magical Circle in 6 Simple Steps*. Tess Whitehurst. https://tesswhitehurst.com/how-to-cast-a-magical-circle-6-simple-steps/

Wigington, P. (2018, June 6). *Where Did tarot Cards Come From?* Learn Religions. https://www.learnreligions.com/a-brief-history-of-tarot-2562770

Wigington, P. (2019, November 27). *10 Basic Divination Methods to Try*. Learn Religions. https://www.learnreligions.com/methods-of-divination-2561764

Wikipedia contributors. (2020, December 27). *Rider-Waite tarot deck*. Wikipedia. https://en.wikipedia.org/wiki/Rider-Waite_tarot_deck

Manufactured by Amazon.ca
Bolton, ON